RETURN OF THE
STUPID
SOCK
CREATURES

RETURN OF THE STUPID SOCK CREATURES

Evolutions, Mutations, and Other Creations

JOHN MURPHY

LARK CRAFTS
Asheville

EDITOR
Thom O'Hearn

ART DIRECTOR
Megan Kirby

DESIGNER
Meagan Shirlen

ILLUSTRATIONS
John Murphy

PHOTOGRAPHER
Steve Mann

COVER DESIGN
MacFadden & Thorpe

LARK CRAFTS

An Imprint of Sterling Publishing
387 Park Avenue South
New York, NY 10016

If you have questions or comments about
this book, please visit: larkcrafts.com

Library of Congress Cataloging-in-Publication Data

Murphy, John (John C.), 1975-
  Return of the stupid sock creatures! : evolutions, mutations, and other creations / John Murphy. -- 1st ed.
      p. cm.
  Includes bibliographical references and index.
  ISBN 978-1-4547-0284-9 (alk. paper)
  1. Textile crafts. 2. Socks. I. Title.
  TT699.M847 2012
  746.4--dc23

                                        2011047743

10 9 8 7 6 5 4 3 2 1

First Edition

Published by Lark Crafts
An Imprint of Sterling Publishing Co., Inc.
387 Park Avenue South, New York, NY 10016

Text © 2012, John Murphy

Photography © 2012, Lark Crafts, an Imprint of Sterling Publishing Co., Inc.,
unless otherwise specified

Illustrations © 2012, John Murphy

Distributed in Canada by Sterling Publishing,
c/o Canadian Manda Group, 165 Dufferin Street
Toronto, Ontario, Canada M6K 3H6

Distributed in the United Kingdom by GMC Distribution Services,
Castle Place, 166 High Street, Lewes, East Sussex, England BN7 1XU

Distributed in Australia by Capricorn Link (Australia) Pty Ltd.,
P.O. Box 704, Windsor, NSW 2756 Australia

Manufactured in China

ISBN 13: 978-1-4547-0284-9

For information about custom editions, special sales, and premium and corporate purchases, please contact
Sterling Special Sales Department at 800-805-5489 or specialsales@sterlingpub.com.

For information about desk and examination copies available to college and university professors, requests must be
submitted to academic@larkbooks.com. Our complete policy can be found at www.larkcrafts.com.

CONTENTS

INTRODUCTION

When *Stupid Sock Creatures* hit bookstore shelves in 2005, I didn't realize how popular the projects would be among crafters. Long and short, the book had an impact on people that was too big and too important to ignore. People who never felt creative at anything wrote me to say thanks. People the world over sent me photos of what they'd made. I was pretty astonished. Just a few techniques and eight projects later (well, nine if you count ZarZak the Silent Destroyer), the Stupid Sock Creatures had evolved into something bigger than a book. They'd become a phenomenon.

I wanted this book to stand for something more than just a sequel to the first book. I wanted to really emphasize the importance of sharing ideas and what it does to our human community. I wanted to exemplify the perpetuation and evolution of ideas. I wanted to show that humans not only can learn but can use that learning as a springboard for creation.

With that in mind, I sought out guest designers to fill these pages instead of hogging all the attention. For the most part, the designers I invited are people who not only used my first book but kept in touch with me to show me more and more new stuff over the years. The team consists of teens, tweens, threens, moms, dads, and one alien (just to show that anyone can make a sock creature). When I chose the projects to feature,

I looked first and foremost at imagination and composition. Some projects are simple. Some are complex. Some designers have tighter craftsmanship than others.

While all of the creatures featured vary in flash and perfection, each of them is loaded with love, enjoyment, and creativity. My hope is that anyone interested in this kind of art can pick up this book and enjoy it as much as the people who designed the creatures themselves. Don't worry about impressing anyone. Just learn what works for you and do it. Sew up something new and original and give it a story. The evolution of our culture at large depends on you.

BASICS

Welcome to the training ground of this book. Since you probably have modern, impatient sensibilities, I won't insist you read every word of this before starting a project. Just reference it as necessary. That's okay. In fact, I'll even tell you when to reference this section, and which page of it, as often as there is need. I'm just that considerate! If you're a hands-on learner like me, skip this section altogether and head straight for the project you're itching to do. You'll be back here soon enough to digest its content....

The Basic Creature Sewing Kit

See? Welcome back! First and foremost, I'll tell you what tools and supplies you'll need for making all the projects presented here. You'll find the Basic Creature Sewing Kit mentioned at least 20 times, so without further ado, here it is.

Sharp fabric scissors: There's a well-known, orange-handled brand that is inexpensive and will do you very nicely until you decide how committed you are to the fiber arts. Please avoid those all-purpose kitchen shears. They might look impressive, but they will chew your socks to bits without making much of a cut.

General use sewing needles: I like milliners' needles personally because they're long enough for my bumbling fingers to grasp. If you buy a packet of long sharps, those should do you proud.

5-inch soft sculpture needles or doll needles: These are the best needles available for sculpting the boofy, fat Signature Stupid Sock Creature Mouth (see page 32) we've all come to know and love. They also provide length and leverage for tricky ladder stitch attachments. Who'd have thought?

All-purpose thread: You'll use this for general stitching. This stuff is ideal for making seams and lots of small stitches in sequence. I love it in my sewing machine but would rather hand stitch with upholstery thread.

Upholstery thread: Upholstery thread is thicker and stronger than all-purpose thread, and I personally find it smoother and less prone to tangle when hand stitching. You'll use this in situations such as sculpting mouths, attaching buttons, bling, or body parts, closing your stuffing hole, or anytime you want your stitches to be especially strong.

Sewing machine (optional): Socks are pretty easy to sew by hand, so a machine isn't essential for these projects. But if you're devoted to quality like I am, you'll want your stitches even and uniform. Only a sewing machine can do that, unless you're an android. I doubt you are, but just in case, let's hang. I've got a million questions about positronic brains.

Stuffing: There's a wide variety of stuffing options for your creatures—see page 10.

Pins: Use long ones with big, round, colored heads. It doesn't matter if the heads are glass or plastic as long as they are nice and visible. It's important that your pins are easy to see; otherwise one might disappear into the folds of your project, and you'll stick yourself later.

Thimbles: Use these to push your needle through stubborn situations. Thimbles make all the difference between stitching and bleeding.

Seam ripper: Trust me, you'll make an errant seam from time to time. This nifty little tool will teach you a lesson for sure. Its simple concept belies its tedious employ.

Craft knife: They're not just for trimming cuticles anymore. These sharp little blades on nice long handles can substitute as a seam ripper, but they can also cut other materials if necessary.

Point turner: Use the pointed end to gently turn intricate parts of your creature all the way right side out. Use the rounded end to dig the last of the peanut butter out of a jar. If you don't have a point turner, use a crochet hook or chopstick. Implements such as these will come in handy, especially for the new, fingered hand designs.

Needle-nose pliers: Unless you really want to get realistic with your creature's mouth, I don't suggest using these to pull out your teeth. I use needle-nose pliers for stuffing small, intricate body parts like eyes and hands with tiny fingers. I also use them for turning such parts right side out.

Funnel: You'll want one of these if you're using beanbag fill. A funnel helps direct the pellets exactly where you want them to go, rather than all over your work space and floor.

Alright, that's it for the Basic Creature Sewing Kit. You might not wind up using all those items, and you'll eventually edit that lineup to suit your own sock creature style.

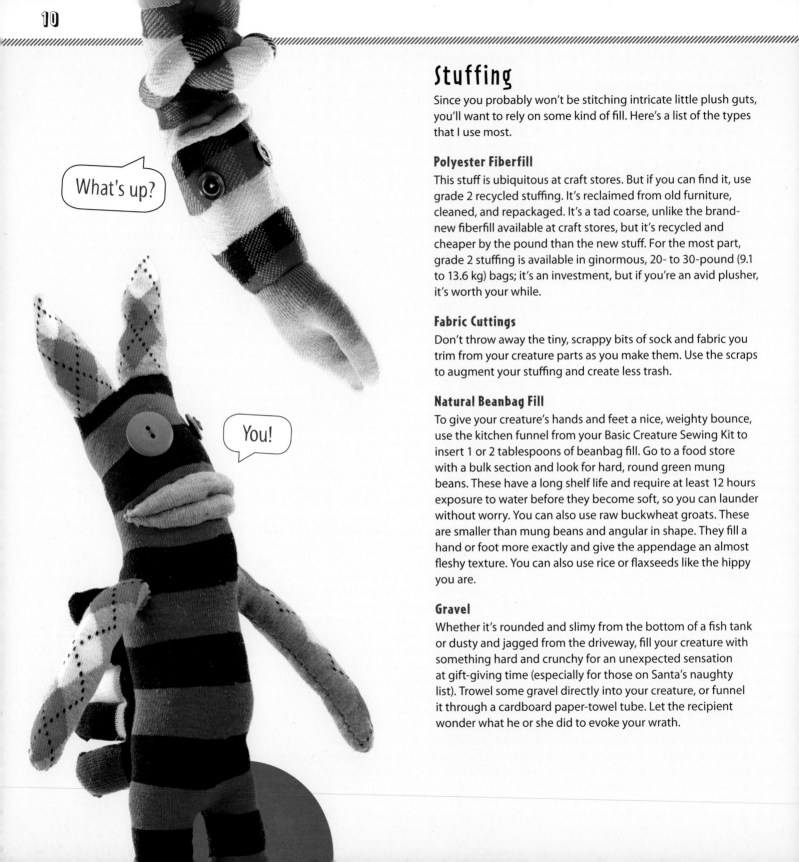

What's up?

You!

Stuffing

Since you probably won't be stitching intricate little plush guts, you'll want to rely on some kind of fill. Here's a list of the types that I use most.

Polyester Fiberfill

This stuff is ubiquitous at craft stores. But if you can find it, use grade 2 recycled stuffing. It's reclaimed from old furniture, cleaned, and repackaged. It's a tad coarse, unlike the brand-new fiberfill available at craft stores, but it's recycled and cheaper by the pound than the new stuff. For the most part, grade 2 stuffing is available in ginormous, 20- to 30-pound (9.1 to 13.6 kg) bags; it's an investment, but if you're an avid plusher, it's worth your while.

Fabric Cuttings

Don't throw away the tiny, scrappy bits of sock and fabric you trim from your creature parts as you make them. Use the scraps to augment your stuffing and create less trash.

Natural Beanbag Fill

To give your creature's hands and feet a nice, weighty bounce, use the kitchen funnel from your Basic Creature Sewing Kit to insert 1 or 2 tablespoons of beanbag fill. Go to a food store with a bulk section and look for hard, round green mung beans. These have a long shelf life and require at least 12 hours exposure to water before they become soft, so you can launder without worry. You can also use raw buckwheat groats. These are smaller than mung beans and angular in shape. They fill a hand or foot more exactly and give the appendage an almost fleshy texture. You can also use rice or flaxseeds like the hippy you are.

Gravel

Whether it's rounded and slimy from the bottom of a fish tank or dusty and jagged from the driveway, fill your creature with something hard and crunchy for an unexpected sensation at gift-giving time (especially for those on Santa's naughty list). Trowel some gravel directly into your creature, or funnel it through a cardboard paper-towel tube. Let the recipient wonder what he or she did to evoke your wrath.

Oh Yeah—Socks!

They are the guest of honor in Stupid Sock Creatures Land. In keeping with the ethos of sock-monsterism, try your best to use the socks you already have. Rifle through your dresser drawers, check for strays behind your dryer, and go raid the local laundromats for fallen heroes. If you wish, you can buy brand-new socks for these projects, but why not give new purpose to those matchless, lonely, single socks you're bound to find? You'll save money and turn burdensome would-be trash into something with a face, which you can never throw away because of all the guilt you'd feel.

For the purpose of instructional diagrams, this book will deal with several styles of sock—and by style, I mean function and length. My diagrams won't deal with a sock's quality, by which I mean a sock's weave, thickness, stretch, and fiber content. A stain doesn't necessarily affect a sock's quality, but its age and wear can. Such things are to be taken case by case. When giving instructions, I just assume the socks you're using are in consistent condition throughout, with no thin spots, holes, or bumps.

In my previous book, you could do most of the projects with a couple of crew socks. My team of intrepid, international guest designers has blown that standard out of the water and straight into deep space. Well, not really. They're just using more than crew socks, and they're doing things with toe socks that I didn't really anticipate but certainly don't mind.

Name That Sock!

Whether it's small or big, chances are your sock is cut a certain way. What type of sock in **figure 1** do you have the most of?

Ankle socks: They cover the foot and go no further up a person's leg than the ankle.

Crew socks: I'm unsure why these are called "crew," 'cause they don't come up to a person's crew. They come up roughly mid-shin.

Knee socks: These go past a person's crew—I mean shin—all the way to the knee.

Toe socks: These little marvels have individual compartments for each of the wearer's toes but often don't have a heel. In my first book I found them annoying and uncomfortable. But I've had a change of heart since then.

Now that you know your sock type, what about the rest of the picture? I'm talking about the fabric it's made of. There are three main categories that I will discuss.

Typically, colorful socks, with patterns and stripes you can see a mile away, are made of a reasonably thin, synthetic material. The stretchiness of these socks necessitates more stuffing to fill them sufficiently, and when that happens, the material becomes a tad sheer. Sometimes, if the sock is wicked cheap, the edges fray and roll when cut.

Stepping up in quality are those ubiquitous white gym socks with the gray heel and toe. I love these because they're inexpensive and well made. They're typically a blend of cotton, polyester, and latex, so they have sturdiness and stretch all at once. I like these for practicing creature prototypes. And you get not one texture, but two, thanks to the fuzzy interior. Who can pass that up? If their stark lack of color annoys you, read up on dyes and fabric paints and see what you can do.

Socks made from cotton or wool are noticeably thicker and sturdier than the synthetic kind. I like natural fiber socks because they produce creatures that hold up really well to handling and play. They cut well with little to no fraying or rolling at the edges, stretch less than synthetic socks, and can take stuffing without becoming sheer.

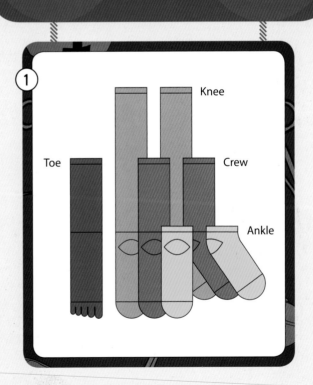

1

Toe · Knee · Crew · Ankle

I'm on the crew socks crew.

Sock Anatomy

With styles out of the way, let's get into some anatomy. Socks, according to me, have five basic regions (**figure 2**).

Toe: The culmination of a sock where the wearer's toes go.

Foot: The part that covers the wearer's foot, and without which a sock would simply be a leg warmer.

Heel: A rounded place for the wearer's heel to snugly go. Not all socks have one of these, but that's okay. You can graft one on if necessary.

Tube: The part that covers the wearer's leg between ankle and knee. Ankle socks don't have much of this, whereas knee socks have it in excess.

Cuff: The folded-over top of most socks, often held down by a row of stitches. Sometimes it isn't folded over, but ribbed and hemmed. Either way, a cuff is distinct from the rest of the tube in color and/or texture.

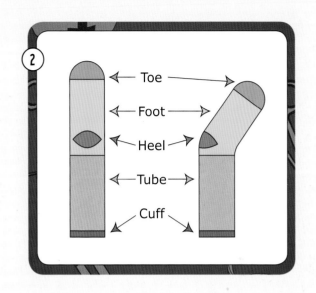

I'll show you what I'm made of!

Toe socks?

How to Read My Symbols

Alright. Now you know how to relate to your socks. We must now learn how to relate to the book. With each of my books, diagrammatic explanation has differed slightly as I get better at doing this kind of thing. Let me now explain some symbols and images you're going to see throughout the book (see **figure 3**).

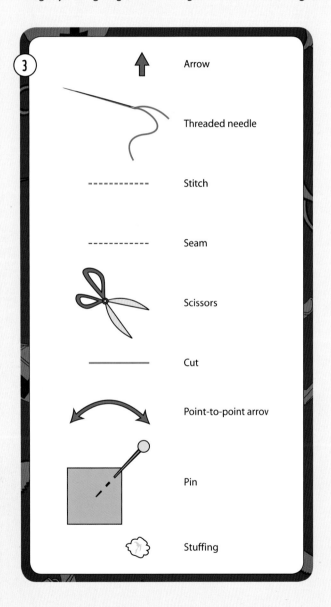

3

- Arrow
- Threaded needle
- Stitch
- Seam
- Scissors
- Cut
- Point-to-point arrow
- Pin
- Stuffing

Arrow: This ubiquitous symbol is used to indicate what goes where and what happens next.

Threaded needle and stitch line: The needle diagram indicates "active" sewing, or the seam you should be making in a given step. A colored, bold, dashed line indicates the seam you're actually making and where it ought to go. This line is never without the threaded needle image, so you should have no question knowing when and where you're meant to sew throughout each step—or confusing it with the cut line. Note that even though a needle is shown, you can machine sew unless told otherwise in the instructions.

Seam line: This line has the same dashed pattern as the stitch line, but it's black (unless contrast is necessary) and skinny. It shows where you've already made a seam.

Cut line: This solid, colored line indicates where cuts ought to be made. It's solid and is never attached to a needle, so even my color-blind friends can tell the two apart. If I thought a diagram needed extra clarification, I included a pair of scissors next to the line as well.

Point-to-point arrow: This arrow isn't used nearly as much as the "primary" arrow listed above, but it's still an important arrow. It indicates where point A attaches to point B. There will be times in this book when a picture really is worth a thousand words, and this arrow will be there.

Pin: This diagram is so self-explanatory that I won't say another word.

Stuffing: When you see this little bitty cloud in a diagram, it means you need to stuff the indicated part. The stuffing cloud is normally accompanied by the primary arrow symbol because to me that made it look more like it was going somewhere and less like a confused rain cloud.

Measuring

In a word: don't. I will give some estimated measurements as necessary, but they're suggestions and will likely vary from these projects to yours. Rulers and measuring tapes are not required except for one or two specific parts (like Pongscription Lenses, page 30).

Cutting

Each project will begin with a diagram showing all the required socks, complete with cut lines. The diagram goes on to show which parts you'll keep and which you should scrap or save for other projects. Use it together with the parts overview to see the intended results of all your cuts (see **figure 4**).

Pay attention to the color of the cutting diagrams. The fully colored parts are the ones you should keep. The faded parts should be saved for other projects or used for stuffing scraps. Oh—and a cut line across a sock means you should cut through both layers unless instructed otherwise. Likewise, a cut line at the sock's edge means you should cut the edge where indicated.

All I want to cut is pie!

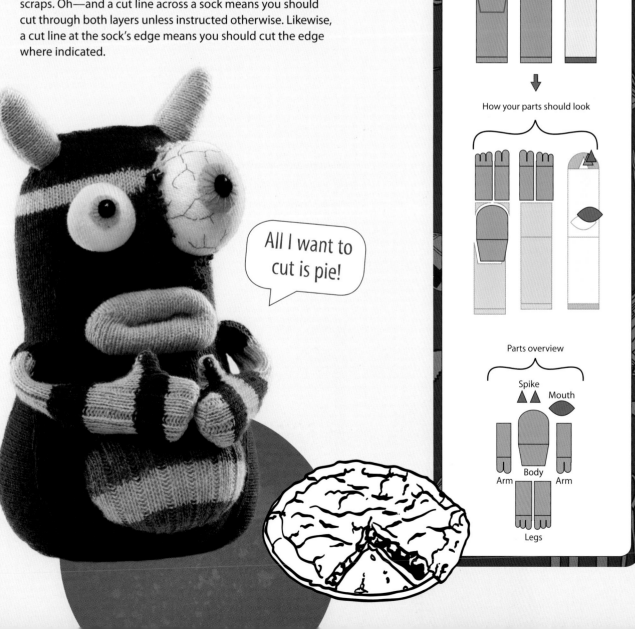

4

Where you should cut

How your parts should look

Parts overview

Spike

Mouth

Arm   Body   Arm

Legs

I'm ready!

You can't sew with that!

Sewing

I expect each reader to hand sew or use a sewing machine at their discretion. That said, some of the projects will require more hand sewing than machine sewing, especially if a body part is attached externally with a ladder stitch. Projects such as Rainbow Dribble, Pie Thagorus, and Morv and Goper require hand stitching for various body parts.

As you sew, it is essential to bear in mind the seam allowance and what to do with it. The seam allowance is the fabric between the raw, cut edge of your sock material and the seam you're making (see **figure 5**). Usually the width of the seam allowance increases or decreases based on the weave of the sock material. Looser weaves or knit socks need a wider seam allowance. Socks with tighter weaves can get away with a narrower seam allowance. Since the fabric at the raw edge of most every sock material is prone to fray or roll, a seam allowance gives the edge a chance to get all the fraying out of its system before bumping up against your seam. In this book, a ¼-inch (.6 cm) seam allowance is going to be standard. Use ⅜ inch (.95 cm) or more if you need it.

Once you've made a seam allowance, there will inevitably be curves and corners to contend with. For your creature to turn right side out the right way, you'll need to notch the seam allowance on concave curves, and trim the seam allowance at the corners of things. See **figure 6** for examples of when to notch, and **figure 7** for examples of when to trim.

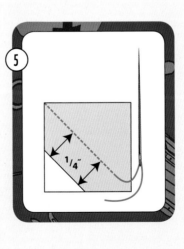

5

1/4"

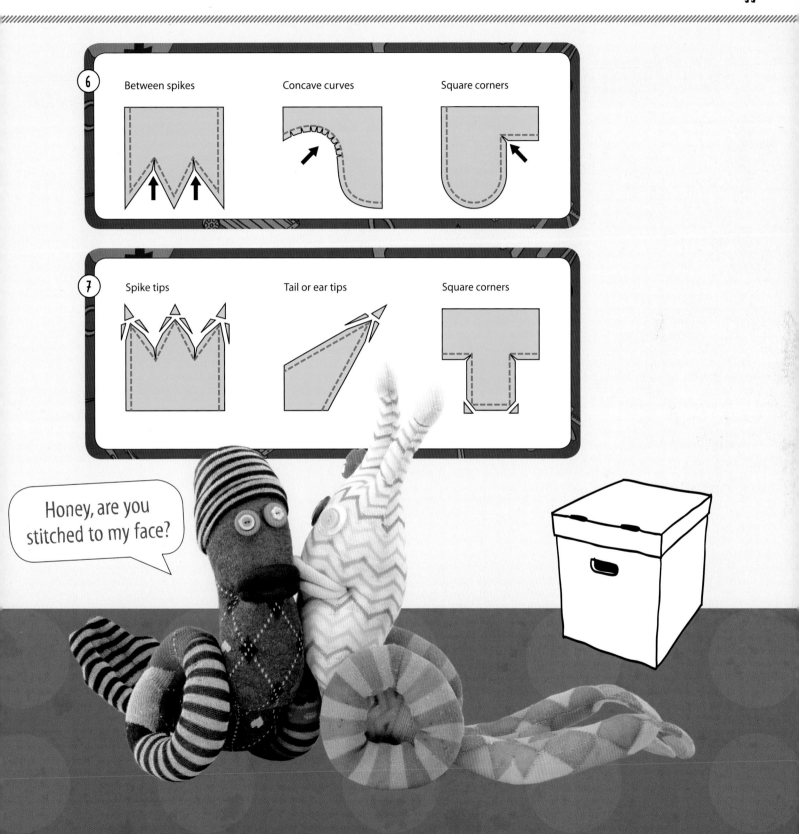

Stitch It

ON THE MACHINE

Straight stitch: Go ahead and make this stitch your default. Set your length to 2 or 3 and your width to 0, and you should be golden.

Zigzag stitch: Use this stitch if your sock material is loosely woven or prone to fray. Set your width to 4 and your length to 3. Vary those settings as necessary.

BY HAND

Anchoring knot (figure 8): I use this knot for anchoring my thread into place before starting a hand-sewn seam. It's a bastardized French knot, which is primarily a decoration. I use this also when tying off my thread after I've finished a seam.

Backstitch (figure 9): I recommend this as your default stitch for making seams. If done properly and evenly, the stitch allows for its own ease when stuffing.

Overcast stitch (figure 10): Some people call it a whipstitch. This is a great stitch for beginner sewers. It's ideal for sock fabrics that are prone to fray because it binds the edges as you go.

Running stitch (figure 11): Some people call this a basting stitch. It can be used in place of pins for holding fabric loosely together until you stitch it for real. But in this book, it will be used as kind of a drawstring to cinch openings of body parts smaller before attaching them to the body. Use long and loose stitches, and don't pull the stitches tight as with other techniques.

Ladder stitch (figure 12): I use this stitch for attaching body parts externally and for closing up stuffing holes. When done properly, it kind of tucks away and hides itself between layers of fabric. It's a tad tricky to do, so I recommend looking up some video tutorials on how to do it. When you get it right, you will love it.

ON THE MACHINE OR BY HAND

Topstitch: Topstitching, used ubiquitously in quilting, both decorates and stabilizes the layers of a sewn project. It's done by running a straight stitch with your sewing machine, or a backstitch by hand through the layers of your sewn item. I use topstitching down the middle of a creature's tongue to give it an authentic looking crease. Kelly McCaffrey uses topstitching on Queegsly (see below left) to quilt body parts such as fingery wings and batlike toes. You'll find plenty of uses for this technique in monster making.

Is there a Mrs. Yellow-Eyed Ugly?

Yep.

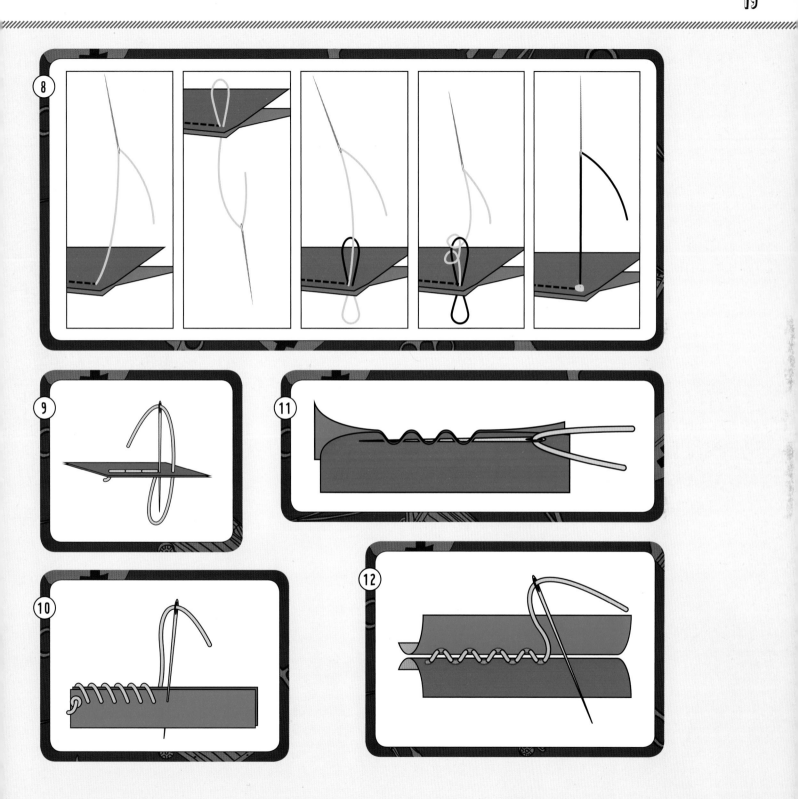

Stuffing Techniques

When your creature is completely stitched and turned right side out, you'll want to fill it out and give it some shape. When a creature is stuffed, it finally has the shape and dimension that give it personality!

No matter where your stuffing hole is, you'll want to fill out the extremities of your creature first: I'm talking about hands, feet, ears, tails, or any appendage that's attached via the circumference method (see page 21). If you're using beanbag fill in these extremities, scrunch up your creature enough to get the spout of a funnel into the appendage's opening, and pour the pellets down into it that way. Stuffing the extremity as usual will hold the pellets in place.

When the appendages are stuffed, begin filling out the creature starting with the areas farthest away from the stuffing hole. Use moderately sized fistfuls of stuffing and pack the creature evenly and as firmly as you like. Scrunching and wadding your stuffing will create lumps—so will cramming too much stuffing in at once. If you're using bits of sock scrap and other fabric you'd otherwise throw away, add that to your fistfuls of stuffing as you go. When you've got your creature filled out and even, close up your stuffing hole with a ladder stitch.

When your creature is completely stuffed and closed, you can squish it around to distribute the stuffing if necessary. Sock fibers will relax over time, and your creature will feel more pliant and soft within a few hours. If you're using gravel as stuffing, however, your creature will never become soft. In fact, after significant handling, its stitches might rupture and you'll have a mess to clean up. Still, this book is about new ideas after all.

Attaching Things to Other Things

That should cover what you need to know about sewing and structural techniques. I'll now take you through some anatomical techniques that, if not universal, are at least shared by more than one creature. Let's put stuff together!

Circumference Method

This is one of my favorite attachment methods because it allows add-on body parts to be stuffed later, at the same time the body is. It's pretty easy—and with a little practice you can even do it on the sewing machine. Try it by hand first though.

You'll need an unstuffed, finished limb or body part, and a creature that's wrong side out. Decide where on your creature's body you want the limb to go, and use your scissors to snip just a few fibers of sock material there. Insert the tip of your scissors into this cut and open the scissors just enough to pry the hole open a tad wider. Keep snipping fibers and prying the hole wider until it's just large enough to receive the open end of the limb. I will refer to this process as snipping and prying. It's important to make a hole in a sock this way because the material can unravel at the slightest touch. You don't want to cut a limb hole to size, and then have it unravel bigger than you need it. You can always make a hole bigger, but making it smaller again would require a wand and a spell.

Insert the limb, closed-end first, into the body, aligning the opening of the limb with the slit you pried open. Stitch around the circumference of the two aligned edges (**figure 13**).

Insightful.

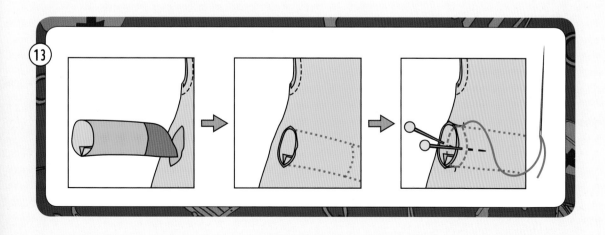

(13)

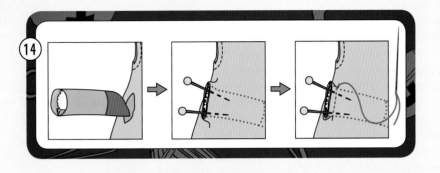

Slit Method

This method is almost exactly like the circumference method, but with a few fundamental differences.

You'll need a stuffed, finished limb or body part of some sort, and a creature that's wrong side out. Snip and pry a slit big enough to receive the limb. Insert the stuffed limb, closed end first, into the slit in the body. Line the open edge of the limb with the edge of the slit. Pinch the lined-up edges of the slit and the limb together, and pin those layers to hold them in place. Stitch all four layers together, closing off both the slit and the limb opening **(figure 14)**.

When you turn the body right side out, the finished limb should hang freely, with all evidence of attachment concealed within.

Vee Method

The vee method is similar to the circumference method in that you'll wind up with a limb or other body part that you stuff when it's time to stuff the body. It's really pretty easy, and **figure 15** should confirm that.

It starts with a design that requires the entire back or side of a creature to be significantly opened with a slit. So what you'll need is a creature with a massive slash somewhere in it as part of its design process. You'll also need the arm, tail, or appendage to attach to your creature.

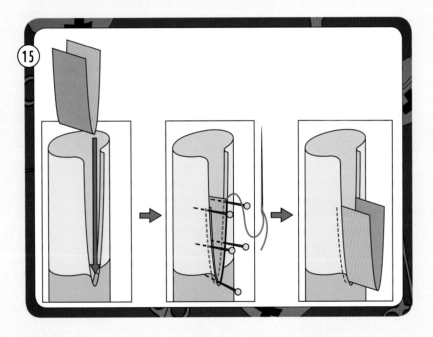

Turn your unfinished creature wrong side out. Open up the slash in your creature so that it looks like a letter V (thus the name of the technique). Keep the unattached body part right side out. Fold it in half and insert it into the slash. Match the edge of the body part to the edge of the V. The fold of the body part should touch the point of the V. Pin the items together there and throughout the matched edges as necessary.

Stitch the matched edges together down one side of the V, and up the other. Pull the body part out of the creature, turning it wrong side out. All you need to do now is stitch what's left of the slash, plus the unsewn edge of the body part, shut in one swoop.

Trap it in a Seam Method

Imagine you're making a sandwich in which the front and back of your creature are the bread, and the part you wish to attach is the tasty stuff you want to eat in between.

Make sure your "bread" has its right sides facing together **(figure 16)**. Insert the tasty stuff, closed end first, between the slices. Match up the edges (crusts?) of the proverbial bread with the edge of the tasty innards. Stitch down those matched edges, thus trapping all the layers in one seam. Do not try this with real food. I will not be held liable for any damage you do to your sewing machine.

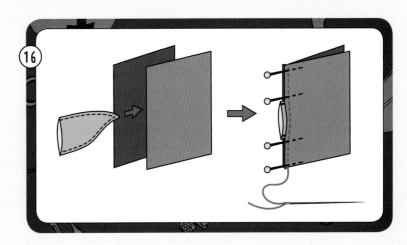

Ladder-stitch method

To attach a body part using a ladder stitch, first you'll need a creature that's otherwise finished, stuffed, and closed, and a body part that is also sewn and stuffed.

You can do a running stitch (see page 18) around the open edge of the body part you wish to attach, and cinch its opening closed if you want to. But I don't find it necessary. It will make things simpler, but I just don't like the way it looks.

Anchor your thread to your creature where you think the body part ought to go. Place the open end of the body part there, and begin using ladder stitches (introduced on page 18) to secure the part into place. Stitch all the way around the circumference of the body part, tucking in the edge of its opening as you go. Make sure to hide all the raw edges and stuffing as you tuck. See **figure 17**.

Making small stitches two or three times around should be enough to secure the item to your creature. As you gently tighten each stitch, they wind up hiding by some force of sewing magic. I try not to question it.

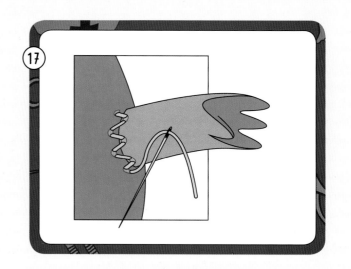

17

Nurse, let's operate!

Darts

Tailors use darts to give contour and dimension to clothing. In this book, darts will be used for giving ears and appendages curvature. See Give and Take (at right) for an example. Simple ear instructions are provided, but Graham endowed Take with a curved ear by sewing darts into the long ear he made. To do this, you will need a wrong-side-out creature with long ears or appendages. Push an inch or so of the tip of the appendage inside the rest of it, as though you were going to turn it right side out. Stitch a curved seam at the fold where you've tucked the appendage in, as shown in **figure 18**. Stitch no more than halfway around that fold or you'll just wind up making your creature's appendage shorter. Continue this process of tucking and sewing at the edge as many times as the appendage will allow, or until you achieve the curvature you desire.

(18)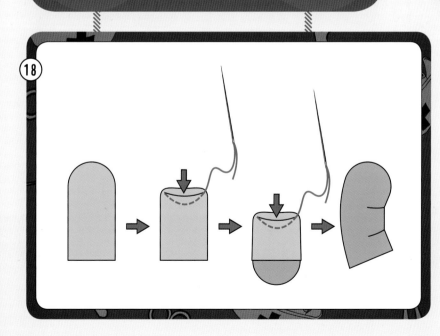

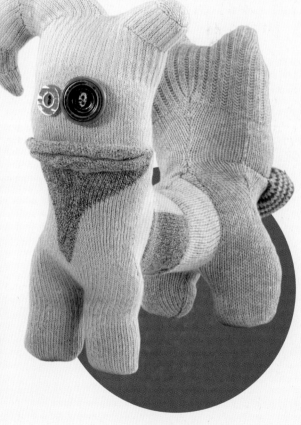

I'll bet your ears aren't identical either.

Add-a-stub method

The add-a-stub method is really the love child of the circumference method and the vee method. It's another way to add limbs to a body, allowing them to be stuffed with the body, but this method requires neither the creation of a slash nor a hole. See **figure 19** for details.

For this you will need a legless creature body with an open bottom, and two tube halves for legs; toe halves will also work. Turn the body wrong side out, and keep the legs right side out.

Insert the legs all the way into the body. Align and pin them where you need them to go, matching the edges of the legs to the bottom edge of the body.

Stitch the matched edges together, and draw the attached legs out of the body. Pin the open edges of the legs together and stitch them. Depending on the design of your creature, you may need to leave the crotch open for stuffing. If you've got another stuffing hole someplace else, stitch the crotch shut as you stitch up the legs.

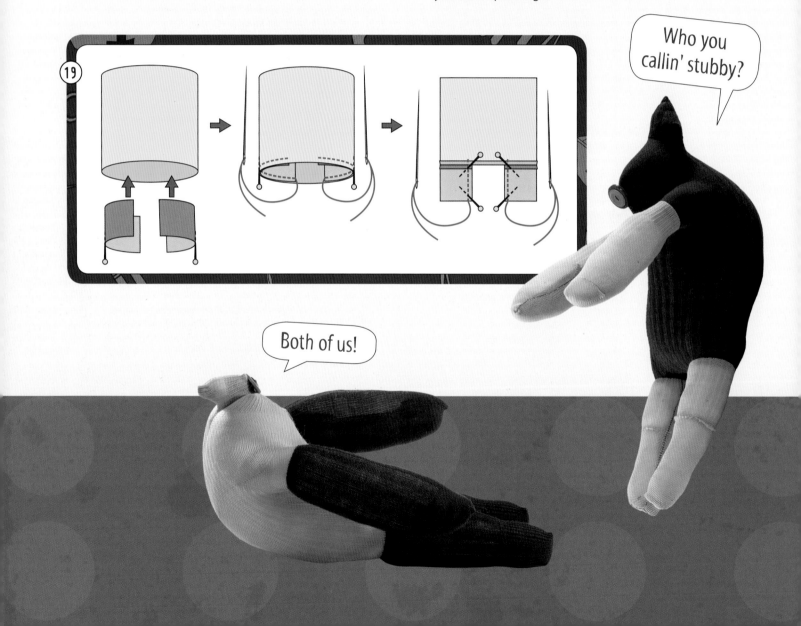

Arm Techniques

The Basic Arms You Know and Love

This kind of arm is the evolutionary beginning of the sock creature arms I designed a million years ago. It's the simplest way to give your creature limbs, and though it lacks fingers, it's really everything you need for the right visual effect. See **figure 20** for the very few steps these arms will take.

With the tube of a sock you can make these arms as short or as long as you want. Cut the tube into vertical halves and turn them wrong side out. Stitch down the cut edges of the tube halves, and stitch a curve across the bottom toward the fold.

And there you go. Turn the arm right side out and attach it to your creature.

Armed and dangerous.

Jabby Hands

These hands are pretty simple, and they do the trick. I like that there's a bit of curve to them and a semblance of a shoulder. Follow **figure 21** to make this kind of hand. Bear in mind there are two variations based on what sock parts you're using to make them.

You will need a section of tube or a section of foot, including the toe. Whichever section you use, cut it into two vertical halves. Turn the section wrong side out. If you're using a toe section, it already has a built-in shoulder because of its natural curvature. If you're using a tube section, make a shoulder by stitching a curve across the top from the open edges to the fold. The rest of the steps are the same whether you're using tube or toe for your arm.

Start a seam at the open edges of your arm about an inch or so below the top of the shoulder, and stitch all the way down the side to the bottom of the arm.

Turn the arm seam side up and flatten it. Stitch jagged fingers at the bottom. Trim and notch between the fingers and turn your arm right side out. Attach it to your creature using whatever method you want.

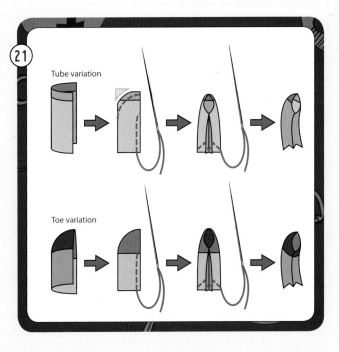

Tube variation

Toe variation

Nabby Hands

These hands were a fun invention and kind of show some evolutionary progress toward opposable thumbs.

What you'll need is the majority of the foot of a sock, including the toe. Cut it into vertical halves, and turn one of the sections wrong side out. Closely follow **figure 22** as you make this kind of hand.

Push the toe of that section down inside the rest of it, making kind of a letter M. Squish all the open edges together as shown in the diagram, and pin. The letter M should now be a letter Y. Pin the Y at its top corners and at the place where all those edges intersect. Stitch each of the three branches of the Y from the intersection to the outer edges.

Next, turn the arm seam side down and flatten the stitched-up toe section until it fans out as shown in the diagram. It will take some futzing and manipulation, but it will work. The shape in the diagram is pretty general, but your results should be reasonably similar.

Stitch nubby little finger shapes into the fanned-out toe. Stitch as many as you are able to confidently fit on your particular piece of sock. Notch between the fingers and trim all the corners. Turn the hand right side out and attach it to your creature by whatever means you think is best.

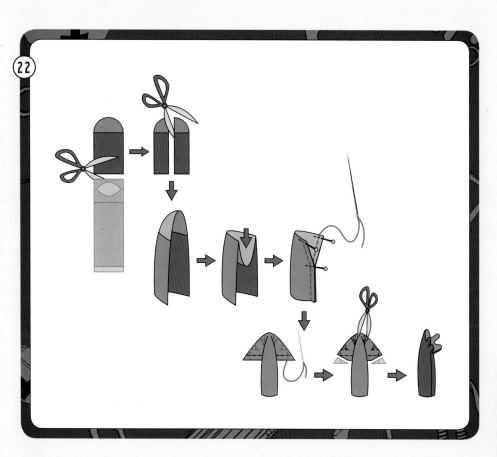

22

Nabby nabby!

If you want to sew a fun creature with nabby hands, meet Blinkubus Jackson at www.larkcrafts.com/bonus.

Grabby Hands

I wanted to introduce these hands in my second book, *Closet Monsters*, but deadlines got the better of me. These hands are really great because without a rocket science degree you can make a hand with opposable thumbs from only one strip of fabric. That said, what you'll need is a long strip of sock taken from the tube of a knee or crew sock.

Fold the strip in half, short end to short end, with right sides touching. Pinch a small fold in one layer. This fold will form a thumb. Pay close attention to **figure 23** because the stitching has to be done in a particular sequence.

First, pin the finger and thumb folds at their corners and at the points where they meet. Stitch one side of the fingers from the fold to the crease where it meets the thumb. Stop there.

Next, swing the arm portion of this limb out of the way so you don't catch it in your stitches. Stitch one side of the thumb from the place where it meets the fingers to its fold. Stop there and trim your thread. Move along the edge of the thumb about a third of the way towards the un-sewn opposite edge. Stitch a seam from the fold of the thumb to the crease where it meets the fingers. Turn and stitch along that crease, and stop at the opposite edge. You will have made a right angle or an L.

Trim the extra material next to the thumb, leaving some seam allowance. Make sure to notch the corner where the thumb meets the crease.

Next, lay the whole hand flat. Stitch the other side of the fingers from the fold all the way to the open edge of the arm. Also stitch a U shape to separate as many fingers as you think you can fit. In my case, I couldn't fit more than two fingers when sewing this, or it was impossible to turn and stuff them. If I were using a wider strip of fabric, this wouldn't be an issue. When all that's done, lift up the thumb, and stitch from the base of the thumb to the open edge of the arm.

Trim all the corners of the fingers and thumb, and notch between the fingers. Turn the arm right side out. Attach it to your creature in whatever way you choose.

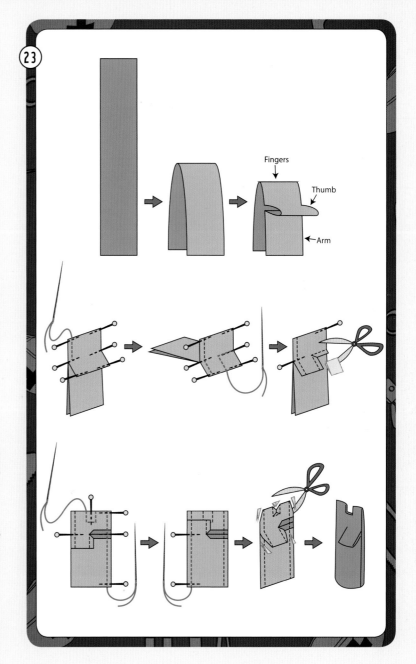

A Word About Feet

What about feet? With just a few stitches, you can create a multitude of different looks (**figure 24**).

Socktometry Lessons

In addition to the classic, go-to button eyes (that you simply sew onto your creature's face), try these new designs, which are an evolutionary leap forward—and child friendly!

Pongscription Lenses

Guest designer Kathryn Odell blessed us with these incredible eyes. They give a creature a really nifty cartoonlike quality (like the Glensphire on the left side of page 31). To make them, see **figure 25** and follow these easy steps.

You will need one table tennis ball, two ⅜-inch-wide (9.5 cm) strips of felt or fleece, which will fit your creature's color scheme, and a creature that's assembled, stuffed, and closed up. You will also need a craft knife, measuring tape, and paints or permanent markers.

The length of your fabric strips should be the circumference of your table tennis ball, plus seam allowances. Use your measuring tape to find the circumference (distance around) of your table tennis ball, then add a ½ inch (1.3 cm) to that. Fold your strips of fabric short end to short end. Stitch the short ends together with a ¼-inch (.6 cm) seam allowance.

For one eye, turn the ring of fabric so that the seam allowance is on the inside. Place the ring where you want it to go on the face of your finished creature. Use small overcast stitches on the inside of the ring to secure it to the creature's face.

Use your craft knife to carefully slice your table tennis ball in half right at its seam. Insert one half of the ball, cut edge first, into the ring of fabric you've sewn onto your creature's face. Use your thread and needle to baste a running stitch around the top edge of the fabric. Pull gently and firmly to cinch that stitch like a drawstring until it tightens around the eye. Tie off your thread and trim.

Finish the eye by drawing or painting a pupil and iris, a big X, or a cat-eye slit. It's up to you.

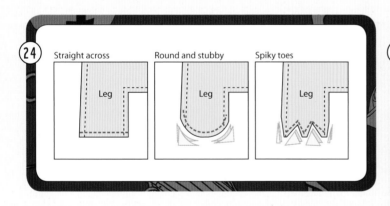

24   Straight across   Round and stubby   Spiky toes   Leg

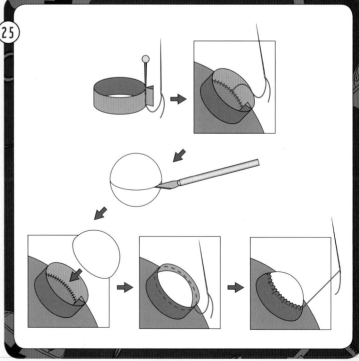

25

Pied Peepers

Another shockingly great eye design was submitted by Louise Revill (see Pie Thagorus, below right). To make these incredible eyes, you will need squares of white (or whichever color says "eye" to you) sock material about as wide as the sock itself; colored felt for irises; black felt for pupils; embroidery floss to complement the color you chose for the irises; and red thread if you want to make bloodshot details.

To make these eyes, lay one of the squares of sock material flat and trim it into a circle. Baste a running stitch (see page 18) ¼ inch (.6 cm) in from the edge, all the way around the circle. Place a blob of stuffing in the center of the circle. Cinch the running stitch closed like a drawstring, encasing the blob of stuffing. Fill the eye with more stuffing if you so desire, and sew the opening shut all the way.

To add an iris, simply cut a circle of colored felt and stitch it onto the eye using tiny overcast stitches (see page 18). Use embroidery floss to stitch multiple times across the diameter of the eye to accent it and give it detail.

Stitch a tiny black circle atop the colored, accented iris using overcast stitches, and you're done. Attach the eye to the face of your creature with ladder stitches or use the slit method (page 22) to trap the cinched opening in place. See **figure 26** for clarification.

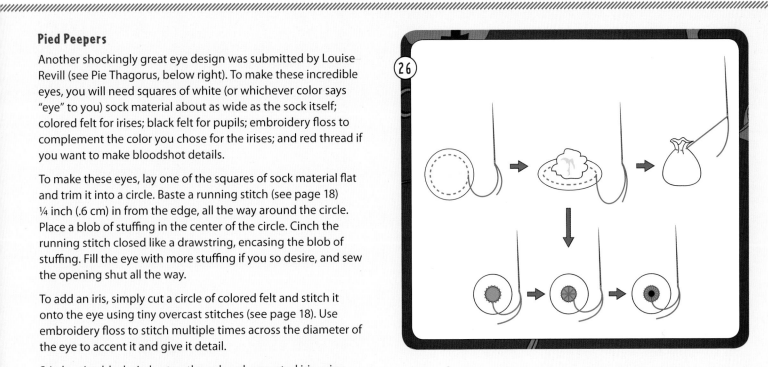

What's he looking at?

Nice to T You

This eye design is one I came up with. These eyes, made from T-shirt material, give the creatures real animated character.

For each eye, you'll need two 2- to 3-inch (5.1 to 7.6 cm) circles of T-shirt material; a small, black snap-on doll eye (4 mm to 6 mm) with its washer, and an awl. If you don't have an awl, you can use the sharpened tip of a pencil or whittle down a chopstick to a thin, tapering point. A pointed tool like an awl is better than bladed tools for making holes in sock material because it pushes fibers apart rather than breaking or cutting them. See **figure 27** and proceed as follows.

Align the circles of T-shirt material with right sides facing and stitch them together all the way around the edges. Snip a hole no larger than ½ inch (1.3 cm) wide through one of the circles. Take care not to cut through both layers.

Poke the awl very carefully through the uncut layer just enough to receive the post of the doll eye. Snap the doll eye firmly into place as shown in the diagram. Turn the entire eye right side out and stuff it. Use a ladder stitch to attach the stuffed eye to your creature's face where you think it ought to go.

I only have eyes for you!

They Can't Yell without Mouths

Sock creature mouths have really developed in the last few years, giving them fanciful new ways to blab and babble.

Signature Stupid Sock Creature Mouth

I really like making the mouths because the creature's personality starts to surface as the mouth takes shape. The instructions for this mouth have confused many a crafter since the first book came out, but enough readers understood the

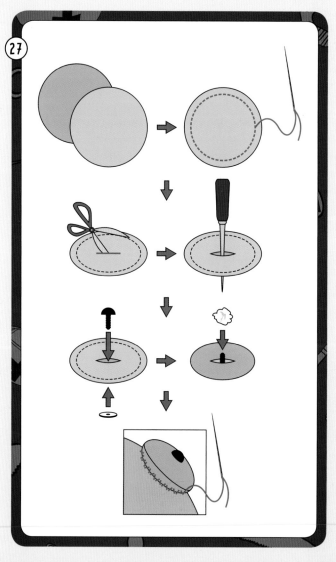

instructions to convince me they're good enough. So take a look at **figure 28** and rely on the creative genius I know you have.

Sewing the mouth is a soft sculpture, or needle sculpting, process. Finish assembling and stuffing your creature before you start the mouth. If you're new to mouth making, stuff a practice sock and work with that first.

Cut a length of thread as long as your arms can reach from side to side. You don't want to run out of thread when stitching a mouth. Tying off and restarting in the middle of a mouth is a real pain.

Now imagine a horizontal divide connecting the corners of the heel. I call it the "equator." Firmly anchor the end of your thread smack in the middle of your creature's stuffed heel at the equator.

Once your thread is anchored, stab your needle into the heel, just above the anchor. Scoop your needle inward to gather as much stuffing as you can. Exit at the top edge of the heel and gently pull your stitch tight. Re-enter the heel at the top edge, about ⅛ inch (.3 cm) away from where you just exited. Scoop up stuffing with your needle, and exit the heel about ⅛ inch (.3 cm) above the imaginary equator. Re-enter the heel about ⅛ inch (.3 cm) below the equator. It might help to press the equator in with your thumb. Scoop downward to collect stuffing, and exit the heel at its bottom edge. Gently pull your stitches tight. Do this all the way to one corner of the mouth.

When you're done with that, stitch back toward the middle of the mouth and repeat the process until you reach the other corner of the heel. Tie off your thread and cut the excess. Now your creature has a Signature Stupid Sock Creature Mouth!

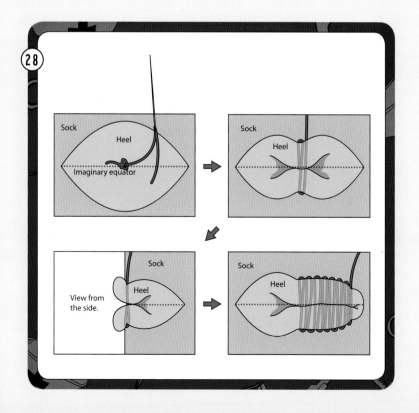

Tiptoe through the Tube Lips

This mouth variation was brought to us by Kittypinkstars (page 88). It involves using a length of sock tube instead of a heel, and it's attached externally. Refer to **figure 29** as you read these instructions.

To make this mouth, you will need an otherwise finished and stuffed creature, and a roughly 5-inch (12.7 cm) length of sock tube.

Turn the tube wrong side out, and backstitch one of the cut edges onto your creature's face where you think the mouth ought to go. Make sure that as you stitch this end on, you're closing up the tube. In other words, stitch both layers of the tube to the face.

Once that's done, roll the other end of the tube up as if you're turning up the cuff of your sleeve. As you do this, insert stuffing into this rolled up cuff (behind the rolled up portion, as though you were stuffing cheese into a pizza crust), and use a ladder stitch to secure the rolled-up end to the creature's face. Stuff a little and stitch a little until the whole mouth is stuffed and attached.

Ad Lip (or Off the Cuff)

Graham Scott Holt and Audrey Farrell use this technique in their projects (see Give and Take on page 35). It's a simple but effective solution that works every time. **Figure 30** shows you what you need
to do.

You will need a finished but unstuffed creature and about 1½ inches (3.8 cm) of the cuff end of a sock's tube. In other words, cut the cuff off a sock about 1½ inches (3.8 cm) down.

Turn your creature wrong side out. Decide where you want the mouth to go, and cut a horizontal slit ½ inch (1.3 cm) shorter than the length of the cuff you're using.

Insert the cuff into the slit, cuff end first. Align the cut edges of the cuff to the edges of the slit. You may need to pinch, cajole, and fidget with those edges to make everything line up right. It's okay to stretch the edges of the slit ever so gently to match the width of the cuff.

Use the slit method (page 22) to close the slit, capturing the cuff's cut end. Turn your creature right side out and finish as usual.

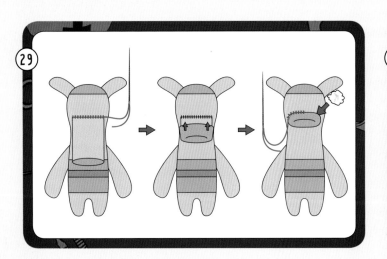

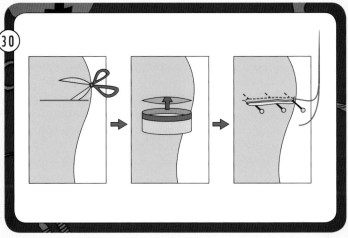

The Wrap and Roll

A tasty feature from Louise Revill's Pie Thagoras (page 66), this inventive mouth method will literally have you rolling. Refer to **figure 31** and read on.

You will need a detached heel or some other ovoid form cut from sock material and an otherwise finished and stuffed creature.

Place a blob of stuffing on the wrong side of this piece of sock fabric, and fold the edges over the stuffing the same way you would a burrito. Use overcast stitches to hold the folds together.

Next, squash a long furrow down the length of the burrito until you get two distinct rolls. Press and manipulate these rolls into lips. On the stitched side of the burrito, make whatever stitches are necessary to hold the lips in a lippy configuration.

Hide all of this work by ladder stitching this mouth to the face of a stuffed creature with the stitched side touching the creature's face.

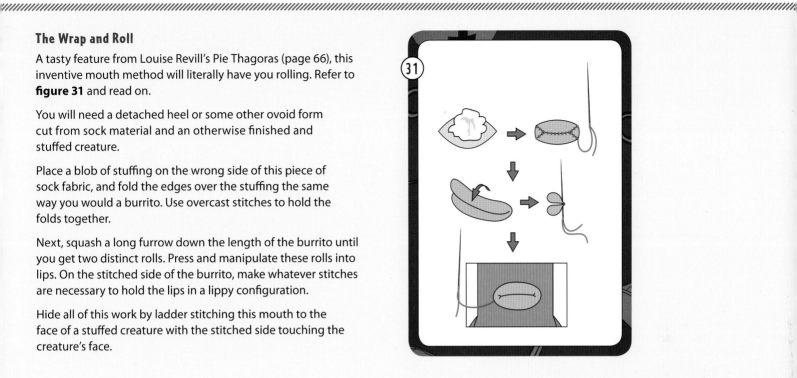

Teeth and Tongues

Now, with all those great methods for making mouths, I'm sure you'll want some info on how to embellish them. Teeth and tongues are essentially little stuffed pockets of sock material clamped between lips. They're pretty intuitive, but here are some methods to follow nonetheless.

Teeth

You can make teeth as individual little pockets, but I like to make them all in a row. This facilitates attachment. Observe **figure 32** for the method.

You will need a rectangle of sock fabric measuring roughly 2½ x 4 inches (6.4 x 10.2 cm). You can cut a folded strip of tube as shown in the diagram or find your rectangle from another source.

Fold the rectangle horizontally with right sides touching. Stitch the short ends shut, and on the folded edge, stitch the spaces between as many teeth as you can fit. The spaces between each tooth should be no thinner than ¼ inch (.6 cm). I allow each tooth to remain attached in a row by leaving about ¼ inch (.6 cm) of unstitched material toward the open edge.

Notch between each tooth and trim all the corners. Carefully turn each tooth right side out. You can stuff the teeth very lightly if you want to. I prefer not to stuff my teeth because they just look too fat that way.

Attach the teeth by stitching the connective bits to the face of your creature before you sculpt the lips. If your lips are added on, attach the teeth before the individual lips are formed, or stick them between the layers of lip (such as Ad Lip or Tiptoe through the Tube Lips) before you attach them to the face. Make sure the open ends of the teeth match up with the part of the mouth you wish to stitch into the face.

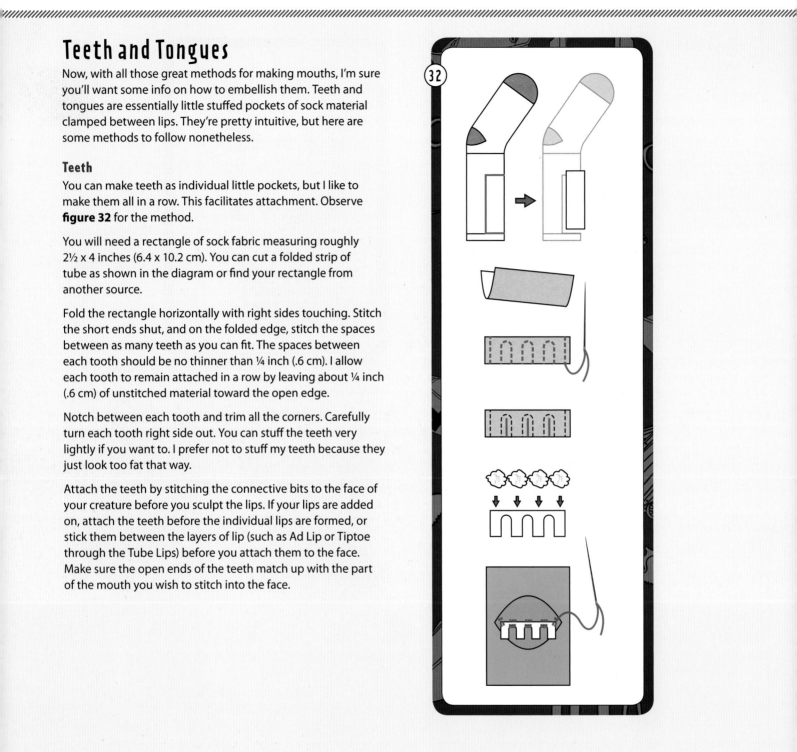

Tongues

Making tongues is pretty much the same as making teeth. You just make a single one instead of a row of them. They look their best when lightly stuffed. Then you topstitch a line down its middle to give it that crease with which we all are familiar.

Attaching tongues to faces is done the very same way teeth are attached. If there are questions, refer to **figure 33**.

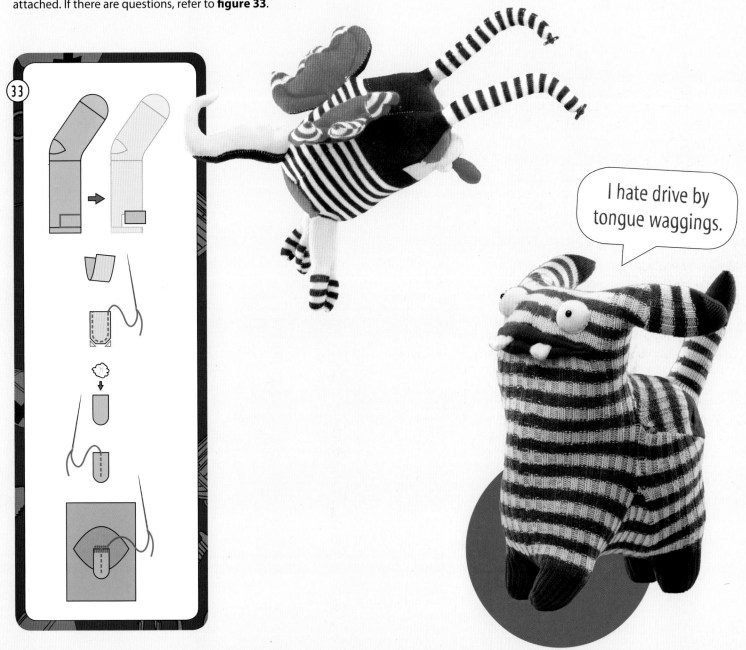

by Jamie Harris

TONY V.

Tony V. is a tremendous sports fan. In fact, it's best not to get between Tony and his favorite sports bar on game night. Those wheels have no patience for obstacles, be they alive or otherwise. His wife is more of a card player, but when she joins him to watch a game they really make a ruckus!

You Will Need

- ✪ The Basic Creature Sewing Kit (page 9)
- ✪ 3 knee socks that are each different
- ✪ Buttons for eyes

Cutting Out Your Parts

You'll notice from **figure 1** that the first sock is left alone entirely. The second sock will provide Tony V.'s tail and hat. The third sock will produce his wheels. Confirm all this with the parts overview in **figure 2**.

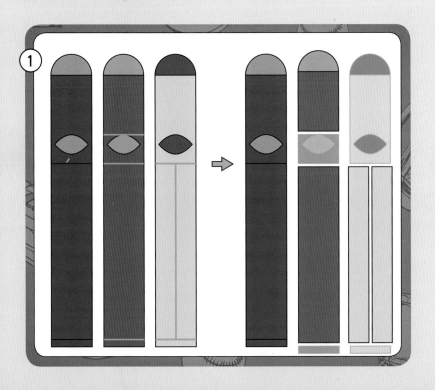

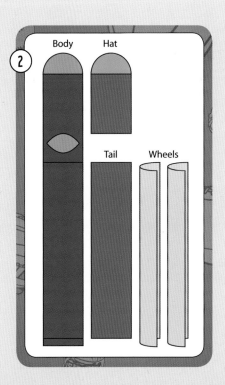

Sewing Tony V.

Take the sock that you didn't cut at all. Thoroughly stuff the toe, the foot, the heel, and half of the tube. Stitch the sock shut where the stuffing stops **(figure 3)**. This is Tony V.'s body.

Grab the part of the second knee sock that you cut for Tony V.'s tail. See **figure 4** for the following steps. Turn the tube wrong side out and stitch a feathery shape for the tail. This shape should take up half the tube. Turn the tube right side out again and lightly stuff the tail shape you just stitched. The tail should stay basically flat. Topstitch some quilting lines into the tail to hold the stuffing into place. When that's done, thoroughly stuff the rest of the tube all the way to the top. Make it nice and fat and rounded, and stitch it shut with whatever stitch you like. This opening will become permanently hidden.

Insert the fat, stuffed end of the tail up into the unstuffed portion of the body as shown in **figure 5**. Bend the body at its seam, and use a ladder stitch (see page 18) to secure the body into a bent position.

Grab the long tube cuttings you set aside for Tony V.'s wheels and fold them in half vertically with right sides touching. Stitch the open, long edges shut, and turn the wheel right side out. Stuff the wheel thoroughly from top to bottom. Do your best to avoid lumps. Bend the wheel into a hoop, and match up the open ends. Tuck the edges of the openings under to hide their raw edges. Use a ladder stitch to sew the openings together all the way around **(figure 6)**. Repeat for the second wheel.

Stitch the wheels to Tony V.'s sides where you think they ought to go; see **figure 7** for some ideas. Use ladder stitches at every point where the wheels touch Tony V.'s body.

Next, for the most difficult step in this entire book, grab the portion of foot you cut for Tony V.'s hat, and slide it onto his head. Roll up its cuff if you so wish. **Figure 8** will ease some of the mind-bending difficulty of this step.

To finish off Tony V., follow the instructions for the Signature Stupid Sock Creature Mouth, found on page 32 of the Basics section. Stitch buttons on for Tony V.'s eyes, or use whatever eye method you think is best (see page 30).

Point Tony V. toward the nearest sports bar with giant-screen TVs and endless buffalo wings, and get out of the way. Root for his team if you know what's good for you.

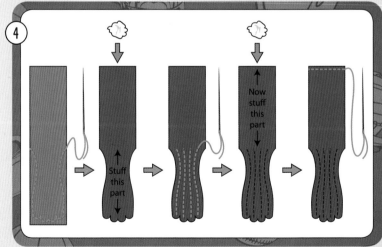

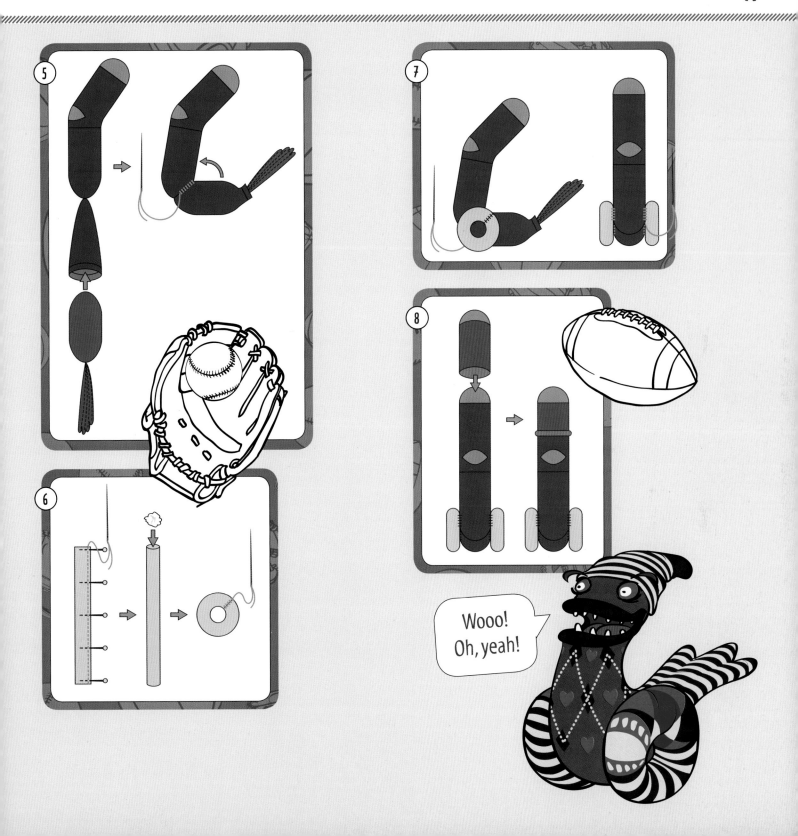

by Kathryn Odell

SNARFLE

The Snarfles were spawned by a particularly nasty pile of dust bunnies. They have always lived among humans, and they mortally detest cats. People who wake to hear grunting and shuffling sounds at night may live with a Snarfle. Their nocturnal misdeeds include skittering around the floor looking for crumbs and shiny objects. Do not confuse a Snarfle's love for crumbs for a free cleaning service. You can count on their razor teeth making short work of your linoleum.

You Will Need

- ✪ The Basic Creature Sewing Kit (page 9)
- ✪ 2 matching ankle socks (with heels)
- ✪ Fleece or felt for ear lining (enough to match the size of the ear pieces you'll cut)
- ✪ Tooth-colored felt, 1 x 3 inches (2.5 x 7.6 cm)
- ✪ Materials for a Pongscription Lenses eye or eyes (page 30)

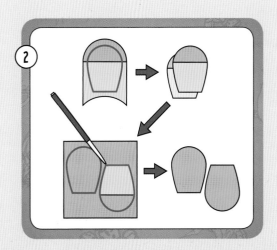

Cutting Out Your Parts

Start with the two matching ankle socks that have heels. To cut your socks into Snarfle parts, observe **figure 1** and imitate those diagrams.

Cut the toe off the second sock (the one on the right in **figure 1**). Remove the entire foot and divide it into four even quadrants; these will be Snarfle's feet.

Next, cut Snarfle's horseshoe-shaped ears from both layers of the toe segment. Trace this shape twice onto the fleece or felt you selected and cut the ear linings out **(figure 2)**.

And with those cut, you've got all your parts. **Figure 3** (page 44) will show you everything you need partswise.

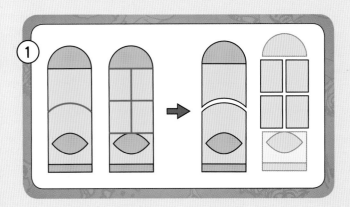

Sewing Snarfle

Grab the segment you cut for Snarfle's head and body and turn it wrong side out. Pin and stitch the curved edges closed. Turn the segment right side out and stuff it firmly **(figure 4)**. Don't make it as firm as a brick, mind you, but this one will need to be a tad firmer than you're likely used to. You want this head to be nice and round like a grapefruit, or a cabbage if you're English.

Once you've stuffed it, you need to sew the head/body shut at the cuff of the sock. To do this, look at **figure 5**. Pinch the cuff closed in the middle the same way you'd close somebody's mouth when you want him or her to stop talking. Make a few tiny overcast stitches (see page 18) right at the middle to hold the cuff closed. Then, do it again the other way and add a few more overcast stitches to hold it all together. Your opening should now look like the letter X. Use a ladder stitch to sew all parts of the X shut.

To make Snarfle's legs, grab the four quadrants you cut from the foot of the second sock. Fold them wrong side out and stitch them in a curved seam across the bottom and straight up the side into little pockets. Trim the seam allowances where necessary, turn the legs right side out, and stuff them **(figure 6)**.

Ladder stitch each of the little stuffed leg pockets onto the bottom of the body/head where the X is **(figure 7)**.

It's time to make Snarfle's ears. Grab the four pieces you cut for the ears. Pair them off, one piece of lining to one piece of sock. Arrange each pair with right sides touching and stitch around the curve **(figure 8)**. Leave the straight, short edge open. Turn the ears right side out and topstitch a seam ¼ inch (.6 cm) from the edge to stabilize the layers **(figure 9)**.

Roll the bottom half of the ear into a vertical tube, making the ear look kind of like a spoon. Overcast or ladder stitch the rolled up ear along its bottom half to prevent it from unrolling **(figure 10)**.

When you've done that, bend the open end of the rolled up ear forward like you're adjusting a desk lamp. Use some overcast stitches to hold the ear in its forward-bent position **(figure 11)**. This bend gives the ears that alert, radar-dish kind of look. 'Cause, you know, Snarfle needs no cat surprises at midnight while feasting on crumbs.

Use tiny overcast stitches to attach the ears to the top of Snarfle's head wherever you think the ears should go, as shown in **figure 12**. Kathryn recommends positioning the ears in several places before committing to a location (ear placement can totally affect the facial expression of a Snarfle).

After the ears are on, and Snarfle is safeguarded against surprise cat attacks, he'll need his eyes and mouth.

Use the strip of tooth-colored felt you selected way back at the beginning of this project. Snip it into a row of connected, sharp little teeth **(figure 13)**.

Attach these to the heel of Snarfle's face the same way you would any other tooth according to the instructions on page 36 of the Basics section.

Follow the instructions for making the Signature Stupid Sock Creature Mouth on page 32 of the Basics section to make Snarfle's lips, and clamp the teeth into place.

Use the Pongscription Lenses eye instructions on page 30 to give Snarfle his eye (or eyes). Make as many of these eyes as you like and place them where you think they ought to go.

And there you have it: one crumb-snacking, nocturnal little meanie for your cat-fighting pleasure. Use these great assembly methods for countless other projects. Enjoy!

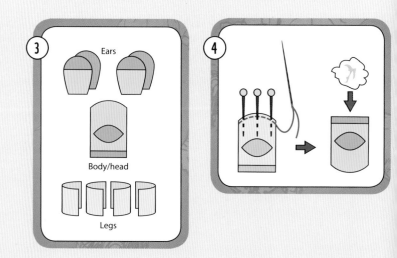

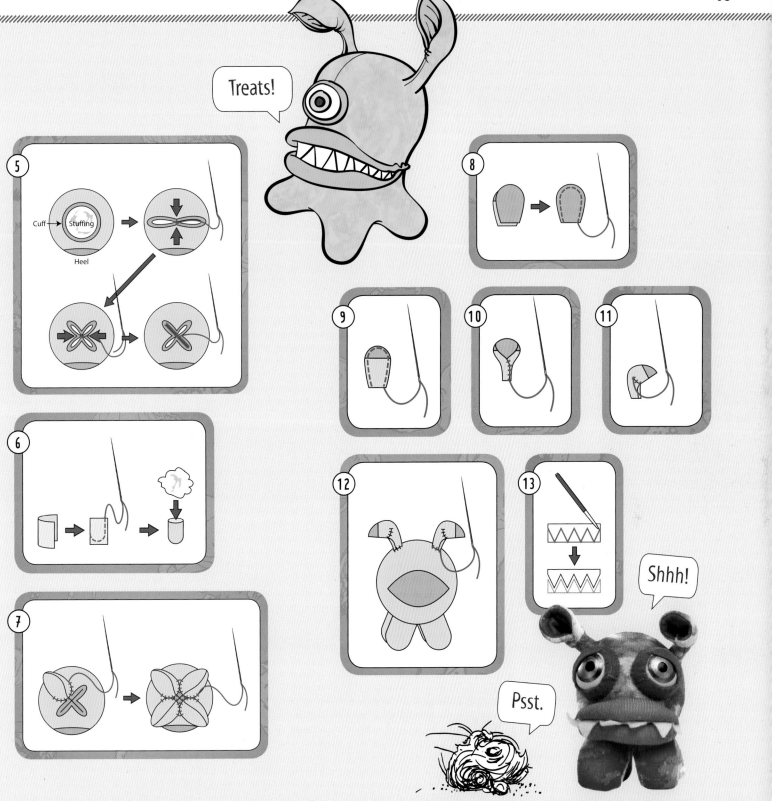

by Graham Scott Holt

GIVE & TAKE

Give and Take weren't always close. In fact, until a near-fatal mining accident, the two were strangers. After the accident left Take dismembered and close to his demise, hospital volunteer Give had a stroke of heroic inspiration. She agreed to an experimental procedure to become part host, part donor to Take.

You Will Need

- ✪ The Basic Creature Sewing Kit (page 9)
- ✪ 2 crew socks (one of them doesn't necessarily need a heel)
- ✪ 4 buttons for eyes

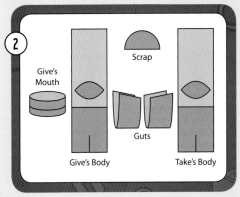

Cutting Out Your Parts

Look at the vivid pink cutting lines in **figure 1** and imitate them. These won't be the only cuts you'll make to your socks, however, so keep those scissors handy.

Give's mouth will be made from a piece of tube cut from the cuff end, so this requires that both socks have the same amount of their cuffs hacked off (roughly an inch and a half [3.8 cm]) to keep them the same length. Both socks will also lose another chunk of tube to make the two guts, and these guts will be cut on one edge. Graham discovered that the guts will attach more smoothly to the bodies if that open edge is cut at an angle. When you do that, your guts will open into trapezoidal shapes when you unfold them. When you've done that, snip a vertical cut up from the raw edge of your tube for making the legs. At this point, I don't advise cutting more than an inch (2.5 cm) or so to distinguish the legs or the guts may connect the two transplant patients at the back of the head. And that's just sick.

Remove the toes from both socks, keeping them on hand for additional material if you need it. Look at **figure 2** to see all the parts required for your little surgical experiment. And there you go. Get your scrubs on and channel your twisted doctor side.

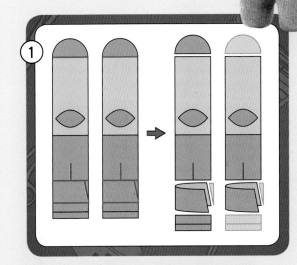

Give's Mouth

Scrap

Guts

Give's Body

Take's Body

Sewing Give & Take

Turn the bodies of both creatures wrong side out. Stitch rounded little feet where you made the cut in the tubes for their legs. See **figure 3** for details. Notch and trim around and between the legs accordingly. Find notching and trimming instructions on page 16 of the Basics section.

Turn both bodies over and make long, vertical slits down the middle of their backs. Stop your cut about 1½ inches (3.8 cm) above the crotches. Don't cut the front of the socks at this time **(figure 4)**.

Put the bodies aside and grab the gut trapezoids. Lay one atop the other with right sides touching, and stitch them together at their shorter flat edge. Lay the stitched guts flat and fold them in half, right side out, with the angled edges touching **(figure 5)**.

For this next step, grab one of the bodies, and keep it wrong side out. I used Give in this illustration. You're going to stuff the guts down inside it. The guts still need to be right side out. As in the vee method (see page 22), match the fold of Give's guts to the bottom of the long vertical cut down her back. Pin it into place and stitch those edges together. Pull the guts back outside of the body **(figure 6)**.

To attach the guts to Take, you need to turn Give completely right side out and stuff her down inside Take's body. Match Take's guts up with the cut down his back the very same way you did with Give, and repeat what you saw in figure 6.

Once the guts are attached to Take, turn the whole mess wrong side out again. See **figure 7** and orient your Give and Take accordingly. Line up seams and points of attachment and pin, pin, pin till someone in Topeka, Kansas, feels a sharp pain down the spine (lame voodoo reference). Stitch a seam down the spines of both creatures, leaving a 2-inch (5.1 cm) space in the middle, where the guts meet, unstitched for stuffing.

You should now be able to gauge what your spleen-sharing creatures should look like when they're done. Ears come next. This step is very similar to making feet for the gut-sharing pair. Flatten your creatures face down, and stitch the ear shapes of your liking at the tops of their heads where the toes of the socks used to be **(figure 8)**.

Graham gave Give some simple, stubby, rounded ears. For Take, he made them longer, and stitched darts (page 25) into the side of one of them to give it a curve. For Take's other ear, Graham chopped it to a nub and capped it with a circle of scrap material from the sock (remember that toe I suggested you keep?). You can do the same as Graham, or you can create your own characters with a unique story of gut-joining horror.

Onward we go to Give's mouth. It's a very simple solution to a much-needed facial element. You can let the cuff flop as though she forgot her dentures. You can roll it back (à la the Wrap and Roll, page 35) to give her a look of surprise. The cuff mouth can do quite a lot if you engage your imagination. To make Give's cuff mouth, first make sure she's wrong side out. Remove her heel, or just cut a horizontal slit across her face. Follow the Ad Lip instructions on page 34 to take care of the rest **(figure 9)**.

And there you go. As easy as getting blown to bits in a mining accident, your gut-grafted creatures are assembled. Turn them right side out and stuff them. Stitch the stuffing hole closed using a ladder stitch. Create Take's mouth using the Signature Stupid Sock Creature Mouth found on page 32, and use buttons for eyes.

Let your creatures roam wherever freedom takes them now that they share an intestine. And may they never have to go to the bathroom.

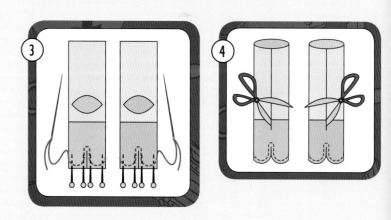

49

by Lizapest Mielke

GOMMEL

Gommel is curious but not too bright. He is attracted to shiny things, especially jingly keys. When not getting his head stuck in stairway banisters, he can be found at the local, kissing cod and drinking Screech. A bartender once told him, "If I 'ad a face like yers, I'd walk back'ard!" Gommel promptly spent the next two years bumping into things and tripping over his tail. Then he tried walking backward. It was pretty hilarious.

You Will Need

- ✪ The Basic Creature Sewing Kit (page 9)
- ✪ 2 matching crew socks
- ✪ 1 crew sock that doesn't match the others
- ✪ 2 contrasting buttons to make a single cyclops eye
- ✪ Cuttings from socks or T-shirts for making teeth (if you want 'em)

Cutting Out Your Parts

So, the cutting for this particular project is a tad intricate because Lizapest just doesn't do boring creatures. **Figure 1** will show you how to irreversibly damage your socks.

The first of the two matched crew socks will provide Gommel's tail, arms, and ears. The second sock will basically be Gommel's body, with a chunk of tube cut off to make his legs a reasonable length.

The nonmatching sock will spawn the spinal ridges for Gommel's back and tail, his face, and four nice circular paw pads.

See **figure 2** for an inventory of all the parts you'll need to make your own personal Gommel.

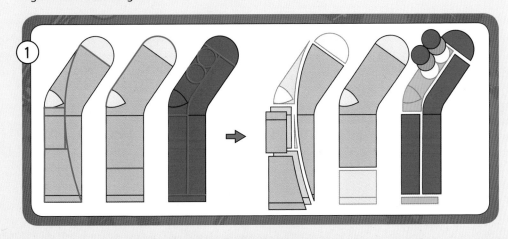

Sewing Gommel

Let's start with Gommel's body. This poor sock is about to have so many parts grafted onto it. Turn the body wrong side out. Stitch legs into the portion of the body's tube that you didn't hack off (**figure 3**). Don't stitch up the crotch, 'cause you'll need an access for stuffing. When the legs are stitched, use the circumference method (see page 21) to attach paw pads to the bottom of the feet. Make sure the right side of the paw pads face upward into the leg.

Turn the body heel side up. Slice a long, vertical slit from the top all the way down Gommel's back to within a couple inches of the crotch. Cut only the layer with the heel on it. Grab the part you cut for Gommel's tail, and attach the wide end of it into the slit in his back using the vee method, found on page 22 of the Basics section (**figure 4**).

When that's done, set the body aside to breathe for a bit and turn your attention to his spinal ridge. We'll go ahead and take care of this part now since it's reasonably step heavy. So, look at **figure 5** until further notice. Grab the two parts you cut from the third sock and align them at one short edge. Make sure their right sides are touching. Stitch the short edges together.

Unfold the long strip of sock, and fold it in half the long way, making sure that right sides touch. Pin the open edges together to secure them into place. Stitch a spiky zigzag line along this strip. Make sure the points of the zigzags stay at least ¼ inch (.6 cm) away from the open edges. Trim the excess material at the folded edge. Notch between the spikes, and trim the points of the spikes. Turn the spikes right side out. You can stop looking at figure 5 now.

Insert the strip of spikes, points first, into the slit down Gommel's back and tail. Use the slit method (see page 22) to clamp the spikes where they need to go (**figure 6**).

Turn Gommel over so his tail and spikes can heal up for a tad. Snip and pry a vertical slit in the front layer of Gommel where you think his face ought to go. Grab the severed toe from the third sock and use that as a gauge for how big this slit ought to be. Remember to make the face hole smaller than the face itself so you can account for seam allowance. When you've done that, attach the toe into the slit using the circumference method (**figure 7**).

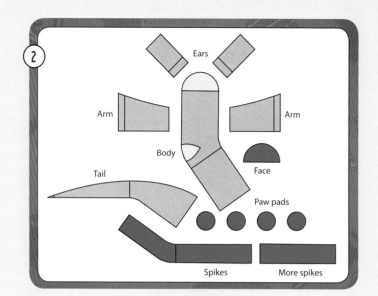

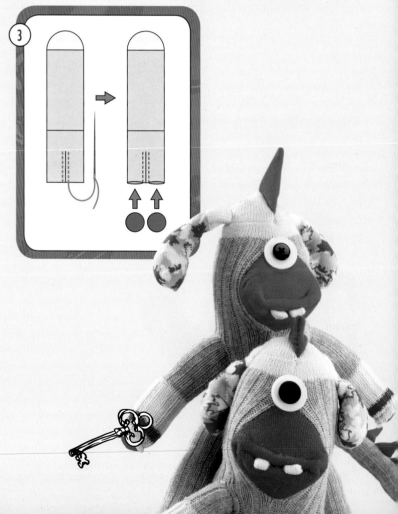

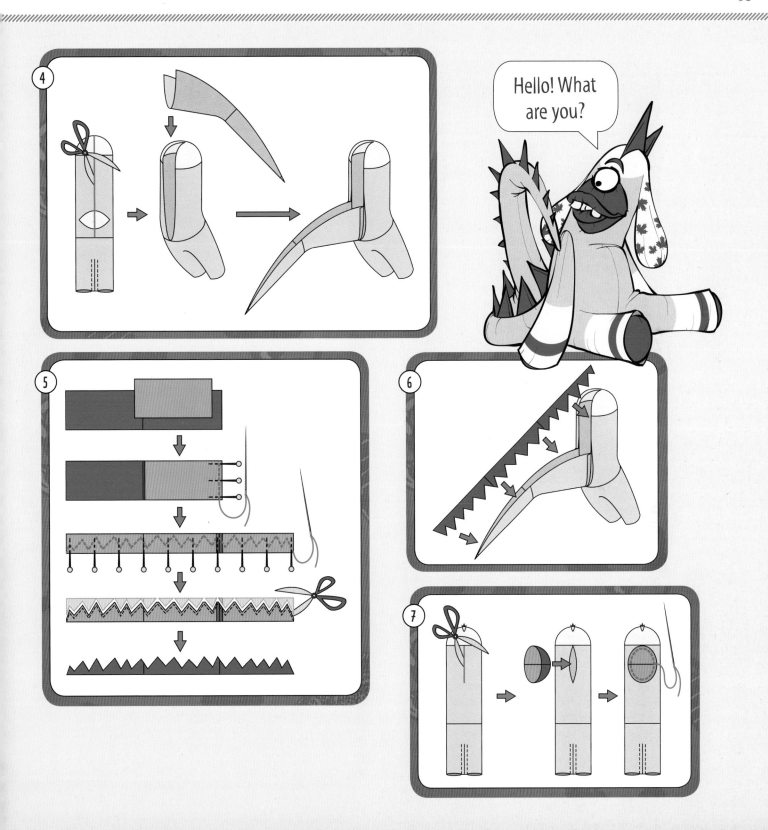

It's time to make Gommel's arms. Grab the parts you cut from the first sock and fold them in half the long way as shown in **figure 8**. These parts aren't symmetrical, but that shouldn't deter you from using them. Try your best to make a symmetrical fold, and where one edge is longer than the other, just trim the excess. Stitch together the long edges as shown in the diagram, and stitch a paw pad to the wide end of each arm. Turn the arms right side out.

To attach Gommel's arms, snip and pry a couple of slits where you think the arms ought to go, and attach the arms to those slits using the circumference method **(figure 9)**.

Lizapest has invented a very particular way to make ears. They remind me a tad of Claude Grénache's ears from *Stupid Sock Creatures*, but longer and danglier. To make these ears, grab the parts you cut from the first sock and fold them in half the long way. Make sure the right sides touch. Stitch one short edge and stitch half of the long edge, opposite from the short edge you just stitched (see **figure 10** for clarification).

Stand the ear on its unstitched short edge. Look at the unstitched half of the long edge. We're about to squash it. You know that hideous face some people make by hooking their forefingers into the corners of their mouths, and stretching their mouths out to the sides? That's what you need to do with this unstitched opening. See **figure 11** if you need any assistance visualizing this.

You'll notice when you do this to the ear, the seams you made earlier will touch. Stitch the "stretched mouth" shut in its new position. You'll have two intersecting seams, like a lowercase T. Turn the ear right side out, and stuff it. Leave ½ inch (1.3 cm) of unstuffed space at the opening.

Whether it's ready for more tinkering or not, grab Gommel's body. Snip and pry some little slits in his head where you think the ears ought to go. Insert the ears into those slits and align the ears' open ends with the slit you cut. Attach the ears using the slit method.

Turn Gommel right side out 'cause you're done sewing things onto him. Stuff him thoroughly and carefully. Stitch up his stuffing hole with a ladder stitch.

Follow the instructions for the Signature Stupid Sock Creature Mouth (page 32) to put lips on Gommel's face. Take care not to turn the whole face into a great big pair of lips. If you want teeth for Gommel, use the instructions on page 36 to make them, and attach them as you form the lips.

Stitch his button cyclops eye where you think that eye ought to go. And there you go!

This creature is among my favorite projects, and I look forward to implementing some of these techniques myself. Hopefully our versions of Gommel will be stumbling backward, tripping over their tails, suffering from the same signature goofiness as the original.

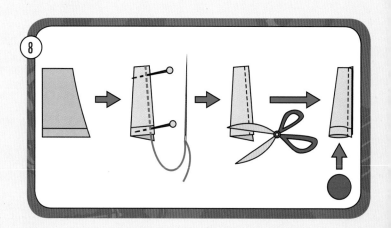

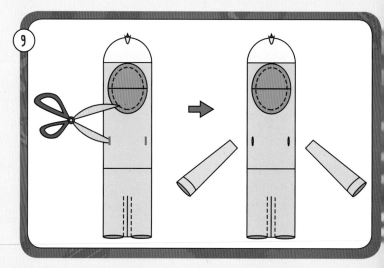

Gommel is my favorite of Lizapest's creations for various reasons. For starters, he's got a heel for a butt, and instead of hands or feet, his paws are capped with stubbly little disks. And the ridge of spikes all up and down Gommel's back is just so...pointy and long, I guess!

by Evan Summers

JUDE

While learning to navigate his surroundings with his brothers and sisters, Jude discovered his voice was appalling and no good for sonar. Now he knows how to play at least seven musical instruments.

You Will Need

- ✪ The Basic Creature Sewing Kit (page 9)
- ✪ 2 matching crew socks (with heels)
- ✪ Scrap of a sock or T-shirt for a tooth
- ✪ Buttons for eyes

Cutting Out Your Parts

Start with two matching crew socks that have heels. Observe **figure 1** and imitate those diagrams. Again, we're not going for exact measurements 'cause that would deny you an important creative opportunity, and we aren't running a sweatshop.

The first sock will produce Jude's body and one of his wings. The toe end of this sock's foot can be saved for another project. The second sock will provide Jude's long, rabbity bat ears, his nubby legs, and his other wing.

Use your imagination to design the shape for Jude's wings. A suggested bat winglike shape is shown in **figure 2**. Cut those shapes out of the tube segments you set aside for the wings. You should wind up with four wing shapes.

Look at **figure 3** (page 58) for an overview of all the sock parts you'll need for Jude. For his tooth, we'll use scrap material from another sock or a T-shirt, but we'll get to that later.

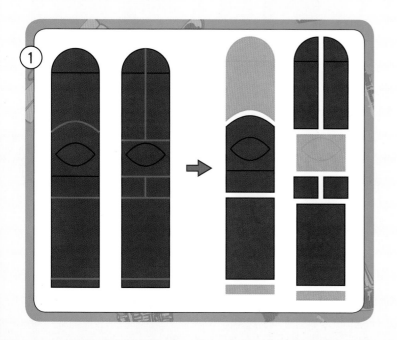

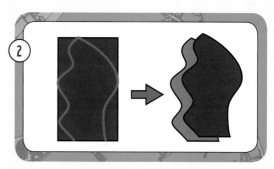

Sewing Jude

Turn Jude's body wrong side out. Follow the add-a-stub instructions on page 26 of the Basics section to attach his long ears. When they're attached to his head, stitch down the length of one ear, across the head, and back up the other one **(figure 4)**. Trim the seam allowances at the tips of Jude's ears, and notch (page 16) carefully between them at his head.

Follow the add-a-stub instructions again to attach Jude's feet. When they're attached, shape them with a curved seam along the bottom of each foot, but don't stitch the crotch shut because you'll need this open for stuffing **(figure 5)**.

To stitch Jude's wings, align two wing pieces together with right sides touching. Pin where you think it's necessary and stitch around the wing's edge. Leave the shoulder edge of the wing open **(figure 6)**. Trim and notch the seam allowances where necessary and turn the wing right side out. Repeat the above to make Jude's second wing.

Look at **figure 7** to see how to orient Jude's wings on his body, then attach them following the instructions for the circumference method found on page 21 of the Basics section. When you cut the holes in Jude's body where his wings will go, always remember to snip and pry. Never just hack open a hole.

When you've got Jude's wings attached, turn him right side out and stuff him. Use a tight ladder stitch (see page 18) to close up the stuffing hole.

All you've got left to do now is Jude's face. You'll start by making his tooth, instructions for which can be found on page 36 of the Basics section. When that's done, follow the instructions for soft sculpting the Signature Stupid Sock Creature Mouth, found on page 32. Stitch buttons for eyes where you think they ought to go. I like doing the button eyes last so I can futz with their placement and determine how they'll look in relation to the mouth.

And there you have it. You've made a Jude. Or a Sarah, or a Binky—whatever you care to name your squishy chiropteran. I hope you have enjoyed this treat of creative evolution! Let it inspire a few treats of your own.

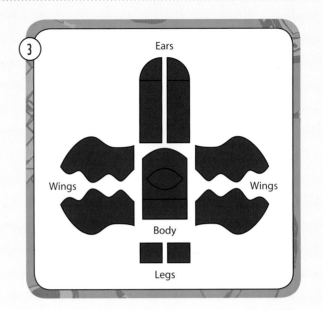

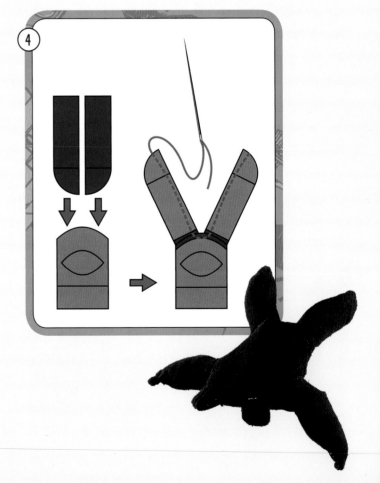

by Addicus Patton

MOOSE WAYNE

Most of Moose Wayne's difficult childhood was spent fending for himself on the trails of Mount Hood. After losing both parents in a tragic occurrence, the young Wayne channeled his anguish into vigilance and protection for every creature in his forest. Now a stalwart detective, Moose Wayne is the go-to moose who takes care of business when things go south. You can always trust a moose with a mustache.

You Will Need

- ✪ The Basic Creature Sewing Kit (page 9)
- ✪ 2 mismatched crew socks of similar fabric quality
- ✪ 2 toe socks
- ✪ Beanbag fill, optional
- ✪ Buttons for eyes

Cutting Out Your Parts

Check out the red cut lines in **figure 1** for the lowdown on cutting your socks to make Wayne. One of the crew socks will provide the body, and the chunks you'll cut out of it will give it the right shape when you stitch it back together. The second crew sock will donate its tube for Wayne's front legs. Its heel will become his goatee, and its toe will become his mustache. The toe socks will provide Wayne's magnificent antlers and his hind legs.

Figure 2 (page 62) will explain the parts you've cut and their purpose. Have a look at it now. Memorize it. There will be a test. Kidding.

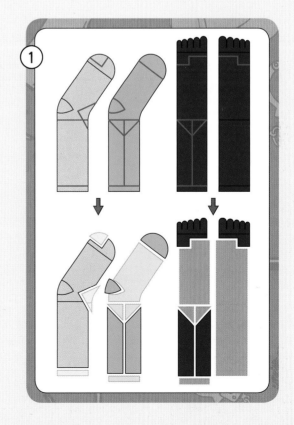

Sewing Moose Wayne

Take the sock for Wayne's body from which you hacked great chunks and turn it wrong side out. See **figure 3** as you do what comes next. You'll want to push the head end of the body down inside the rest of the body so that the edges of the cut you made at Wayne's back match up. Pin and stitch those edges. Pull the head back outside of the body. Stitch the straight edges of the tail as shown in the diagram.

Put the body aside and grab the pieces you cut for Wayne's legs. Fold a leg in half vertically with right sides touching. Stitch along the edges opposite the fold, and stitch a curved edge at the bottom of the leg. Trim the seam allowances at the curve of the foot **(figure 4)**. Repeat these instructions for the other three legs.

When you've got the legs sewn, snip and pry some holes in the body where you want those legs to go. You'll attach them via the circumference method found on page 21 of the Basics section **(figure 5)**. Addicus matched the front and back legs as same-colored pairs. You can do the same, or you can mix and match. Heck, you can even make a third pair of legs with some of the spare material from cutting your socks and place them wherever you want them to go.

After you've attached the legs to the body, grab the toe sock cuttings you reserved for Wayne's antlers. Turn them wrong side out and stitch them as shown in **figure 6**. Turn them right side out and stuff them. Leave ½ inch (1.3 cm) of space unstuffed at the end of the antler so it can be more easily sewn to the top of Wayne's head.

Insert the antlers into Wayne's head. Make sure the big-toe ends of the antlers are touching the sides of Wayne's body so they'll point and hang to the sides when he's assembled and finished. Stitch the edge of the head closed around the ends of the antlers to clamp them into place. Leave the space between the antlers unstitched for turning and stuffing **(figure 7)**.

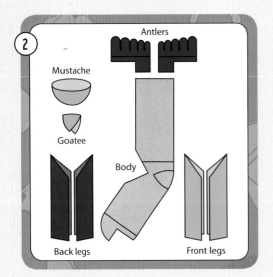

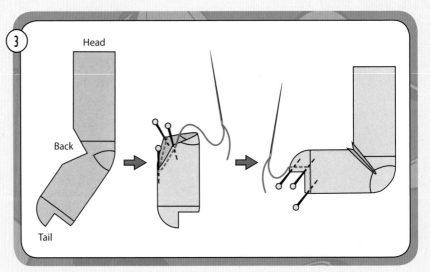

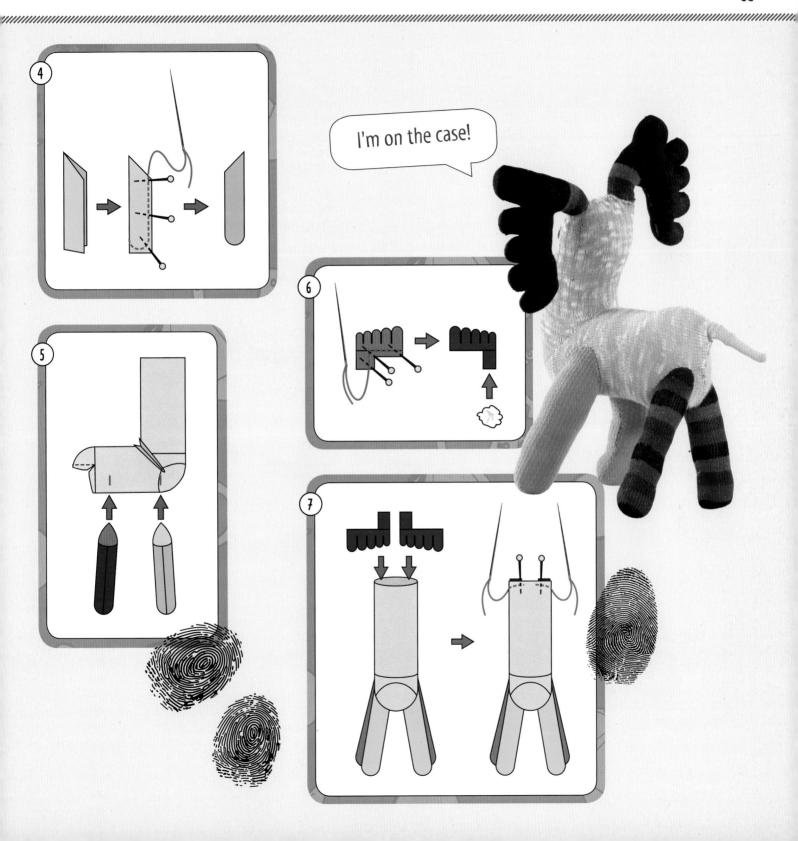

Turn Wayne right side out through the hole in his head and stuff him thoroughly **(figure 8)**. Consider using beanbag fill at the bottom of his feet to give him some ballast and a greater chance of standing up. Addicus's prototypes didn't require this step, so you might not find it necessary. When Wayne is stuffed to your satisfaction, close up his stuffing hole with a ladder stitch.

To make Wayne's swarthy handlebar mustache and dashing goatee, find the heel and the toe you cut from one of your mismatched crew socks. Keeping the toe right side out and open like a bowl, start rolling one edge of the "bowl" down inside itself. Keep rolling till you've made the whole thing a tube **(figure 9)**. This will be Wayne's mustache. It should

have some natural curve to it, but if it doesn't that's okay. You can curve it how you like when you stitch it to Wayne's face. Similarly, take the detached heel and fold it in half with the right side out. Fold its raw edges in toward its center and stitch those edges down to hide them (see figure 9 again). This will be Wayne's goatee.

Use a ladder stitch to attach the facial features to Wayne's face wherever you think is best for your resilient, irrepressible detective moose of the great wild world **(figure 10)**.

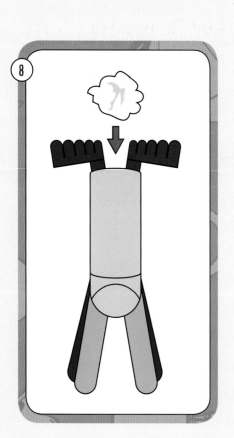

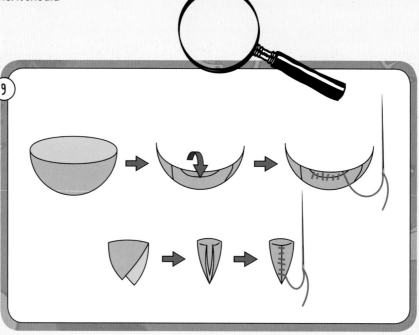

Finish Wayne off by attaching the buttons you selected for his eyes. Feel free to use any of the eye options featured in the Basics section (see page 30) if buttons aren't your thing. The important thing here is that Wayne be able to see. After all, very few blind detectives have made history. If there were a blind detective, I hope he or she would have made history 'cause it's quite a feat to detect things you can't see. Whatever. Enjoy your gangly hero moose and make a whole herd to help him in his vigilant efforts.

The game is afoot!

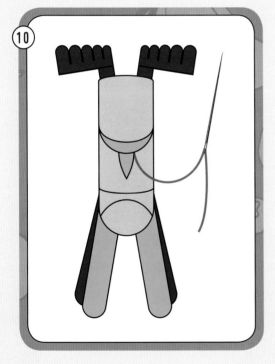

10

In designing Moose Wayne, Addicus used familiar techniques to create a new kind of quadruped. His take on facial features is also new and different for this kind of work because it's refreshingly simple and implies just enough visual reference for our imaginations to do the rest. This project will offer you plenty of new ideas and new ways to approach your own creatures in the future.

by Louise Revill

PIE THAGORUS

Pie Thagorus—PT for short—is a chubby little fellow who likes to eat pies. You'll know he's spotted a tasty one when his eyes pop right out of his head. PT is lazy enough to require no legs, but he expects to be carried everywhere he goes.

You Will Need

- ✪ The Basic Creature Sewing Kit (page 9)
- ✪ 2 matching crew socks, with or without heels
- ✪ 1 crew sock of a contrasting color or pattern to the pair you chose
- ✪ Supplies for Pied Peepers (page 31), including a white sock
- ✪ Beanbag fill

Cutting Out Your Parts

Observe the vivid blue cut marks on the socks shown in **figure 1** and cut your socks accordingly. There will be plenty of leftover material to use in other projects. In fact, there's plenty leftover right now to make a spare set of arms if you want.

From the first sock of the pair you chose, cut the foot off to use for PT's body and head. The slits in the sides of the body should go about halfway up from the bottom. The tube of that sock will produce both of his arms. The second sock of the pair will provide side gussets to give PT his apple bottom and pie gut. The contrasting sock you chose will give you PT's tummy patch, mouth, and horns. The white sock will give you the whites of his eyes. Louise recommends you cut one circle 2¾ inches (7 cm) in diameter, and the other one 4 inches (10.2 cm) in diameter.

Refer to **figure 2** for any additional clarification you may need on the parts required for PT.

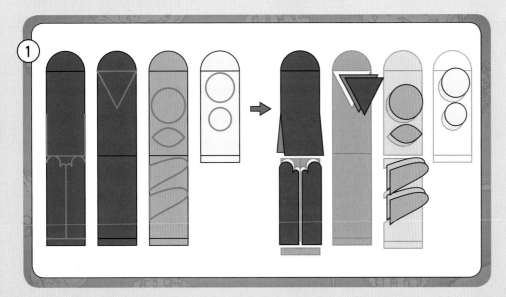

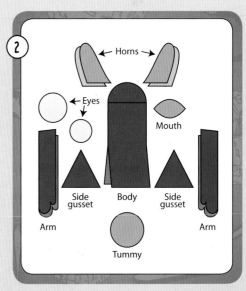

Horns

Eyes

Mouth

Side gusset

Body

Side gusset

Arm

Tummy

Arm

Sewing Pie Thagorus

Onward. Grab the body and turn it wrong side out. Stitch the side gussets into place using the vee method found on page 22 of the Basics section. Make sure these stitches are especially thorough and strong since these seams will hold lots of stuffing at bay. A backstitch is recommended, but an overcast (page 18) will do if you keep your stitches close together **(figure 3)**.

Lay the body flat with the gussets to the side. Cut a hole in PT's tummy where you want the patch to go. Make the hole about half the size of the circle you cut for PT's tummy patch. Stretch the hole gently to accommodate the size of the tummy patch and stitch it on using the circumference method found on page 21 of the Basics section **(figure 4)**.

Next, make PT's horns. Take the shapes you cut for the horns. Align two of them with right sides together and stitch them, leaving the short, flat edge open **(figure 5)**. Repeat this step for the other horn and turn them both right side out.

Attach the horns to PT's head using the circumference method **(figure 6)**. Remember to snip and pry the holes in PT's head instead of simply cutting them.

To make eyes for Pie Thagorus, follow the Pied Peepers instructions on page 31. Louise embroidered some bloody eye veins in PT's larger eye to give him a desperate, hungry leer. You can do the same at this point if you wish. A backstitch is recommended for this.

Keep Pie Thagorus wrong side out and snip and pry some tiny slits in his face where you want the eyes to go. Shove the eyes up into the body and pop the cinched up seam allowances through. Use the slit method (see page 22) to clamp the eyes into place **(figure 7)**.

To get the frayed, burst-eye-socket effect, pry the hole wider in PT's face for the bigger eye. Allow some of the frayed edge to escape to the right side of the body, and stitch the eye on using the circumference method rather than the slit method.

Turn Pie Thagorus's body right side out. Baste a running stitch ½ inch (1.3 cm) away from the bottom edge of his body. Stuff Pie Thagorus thoroughly, and cinch closed the bottom of his body. Unlike the eyes, you must tuck the seam allowances inside the body. Close the bottom up as tightly as you can. Use a ladder stitch to shut what you cannot cinch closed **(figure 8)**.

It is time to make Pie Thagorus's mouth. Use the Wrap and

Roll mouth instructions from page 35, and ladder stitch the mouth onto Pie Thagorus's face where you think it ought to go **(figure 9)**.

You're almost done. Grab the parts you cut for Pie Thagorus's arms. Fold them in half vertically with right sides touching. Stitch a long arm and thumbed paw as shown in **figure 10**. Turn the arms right side out, and funnel in some beanbag fill to give the arms a floppy, weighty bounce.

Tuck the raw edges of PT's arms inside the arms, then ladder stitch the arms onto PT's body where you think they ought to go. And pat yourself on the back. You've finished Pie Thagorus. Now go pour yourself something stiff (or simply tasty if you aren't of age) and start baking a pie before your new friend turns its greedy eyes upon your cat.

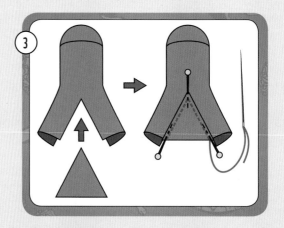

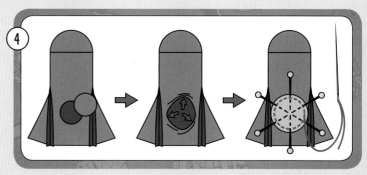

by Lise Petrauskas

SALMAN

Salman is a shy and sensitive monster except when he's dancing to his favorite Bollywood soundtracks. He often develops crushes on emotionally unavailable monsters, which leads to much mooning about. Perhaps heartache is unavoidable with such unrealistic expectations, but we hope that one day he will meet a monster of similar romantic propensities who will love him back.

You Will Need

- ✪ The Basic Creature Sewing Kit (page 9)
- ✪ 1 pair of crew socks
- ✪ 1 single crew sock
- ✪ Buttons for eyes

Cutting Out Your Parts

Salman's got a lot of parts, but it's a manageable roster. See **figure 1** for the cuts you need to make for Salman's anatomy. The first sock from your pair will produce Salman's body and his head. The second sock from the pair will become his arms and tentacle tops. The single sock will give you Salman's tentacle bottoms, mouth, belly, and his prominent cranial prong. Look at **figure 2** for an overview of everything you should cut.

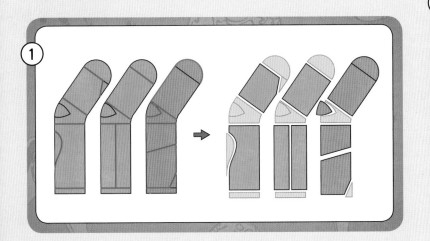

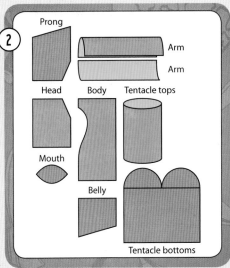

Sewing Salman

Alright. Because Salman is basically a totem pole of stacked body parts, we'll start from the top. If you observe **figure 1**, you'll notice that the head and the prong both have a diagonal cut snipped from them, producing an open edge. Turn those parts wrong side out, and stitch those diagonal cuts shut as shown in **figure 3**.

Turn the prong right side out and slide it, closed end first, down inside the head. Match up the seam at the bottom of the prong with the seam at the top of the head, where you sewed the diagonal cuts in the previous step, and attach the prong to the head using the circumference method found on page 21. Similarly, attach the top edge of the mouth part to the bottom edge of the head. This attachment errs on the side of add-a-stub, so do it that way (see page 26). Pull the prong and mouth back outside of the head (they will be wrong side out). Stitch a prong shape of your choice into Salman's cranial protuberance **(figure 4)**. Make sure you leave enough negative space between your seams to allow for seam allowance. Notch and trim (see page 16) around those seams.

Turn that whole assembly right side out and let it breathe for a second. Pat yourself on the back. You've just finished making Salman's head.

Grab Salman's body and turn it wrong side out. Stitch the neck curve shut as shown in **figure 5**. Wasn't that simple?

Now, insert the head down into the body. Make sure the mouth is on the side of the body where the curved neck seam is. Shove the belly up into the body. Match the flat edge of the belly to the bottom edge of the body. You're not sewing up the diagonal edge yet. Stitch both the head and the belly to their respective edges of the body using the circumference method. Pull them right back out, turning the whole assemblage wrong side out **(figure 6)**.

Time for arms. Grab the parts you cut for Salman's arms and fold them in half vertically with the right sides touching. Pin and stitch the long edge and stitch a curve at the short edge at the bottom for a rounded little paw. Leave the other short edge open for attaching to the body **(figure 7)**. Repeat these instructions for the second arm.

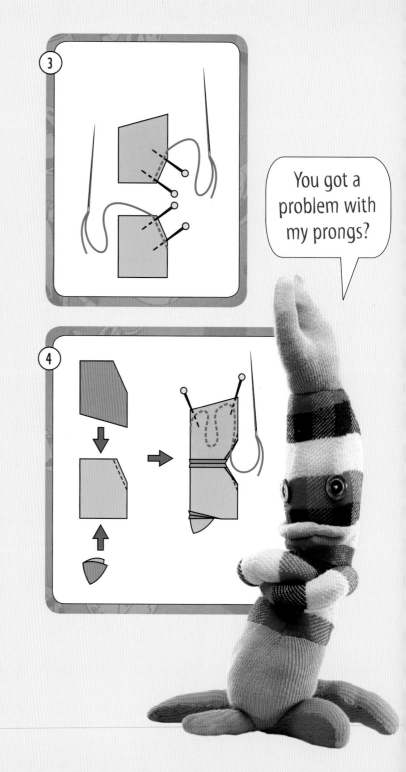

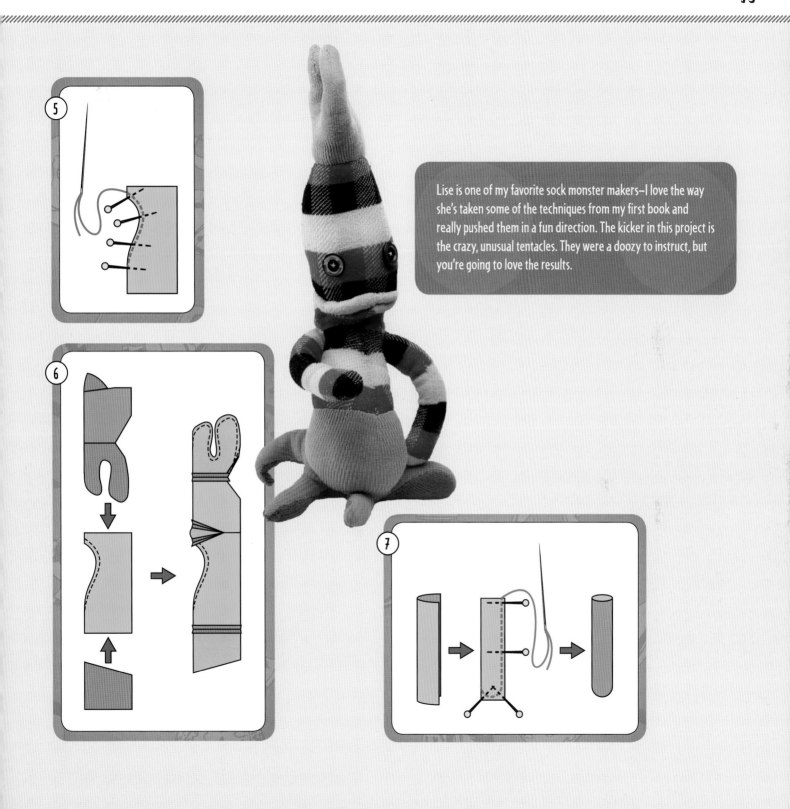

5

6

7

Lise is one of my favorite sock monster makers—I love the way she's taken some of the techniques from my first book and really pushed them in a fun direction. The kicker in this project is the crazy, unusual tentacles. They were a doozy to instruct, but you're going to love the results.

Snip and pry some armholes in Salman's sides where you think his arms ought to go, and attach his arms to his body using the circumference method (**figure 8**). Set that body aside and let it relax.

Okeydokey. Here we go with the pride and joy of Lise's invention: Salman's tentacles. Let's do the easy part first. Grab the part you cut for Salman's tentacle tops. Make four vertical cuts as shown in **figure 9**. Stop your cuts within 1½ inches (3.8 cm) of the top edge. You'll get what looks like a starfish. Lise will tell you it doesn't matter whether the tentacles are uniformly wide; I diagrammed them that way just to simplify it. And Lise doesn't necessarily require the next step, but it only makes sense to me to round off the tentacles' corners. So that's what I put in the diagram. Set your starfish aside.

The tentacle bottoms are a fun thing to cut. Refer to **figure 10** to see what you should do. You need to make five cuts into the tentacle bottoms piece as shown in the diagram. And once again, Lise might disagree, but it makes sense to me that the corners of the flaps you will create should be rounded off.

Alright. The next step gets a bit tricky to explain—and to diagram for that matter. Place the starfish-looking tentacle tops on the mutant shamrock-looking tentacle bottoms and match the corners in between each appendage. Start matching the edges of the starfish legs to the edges of the shamrock petals no matter where and how those edges align. You'll notice that the resulting tentacles will twist and turn and become quite irregular. This is the intended result—and the magic of this particular technique. Stitch the matched edges together regardless of how those edges twist and curve (**figure 11**). Turn the dysmorphic tentacles right side out.

Grab the majority of Salman's body. Keep it wrong side out for now. Insert the tentacles, ends first, into the body. Align the "waist" of the tentacles with the bottom edge of the belly. Attach the two edges using the circumference method (**figure 12**). Leave a 2-inch (5.1 cm) space unstitched in the back of Salman's body. Turn Salman right side out through this opening.

Stuff Salman thoroughly, and close up his stuffing hole with a ladder stitch. Stitch buttons on for eyes wherever you think eyes ought to go, or follow directions for whichever eye you prefer in the Basics section (see page 30). Heck. Invent your own eyes if you want. Everything in this book is a suggestion anyway.

Follow the instructions for the Signature Stupid Sock Creature Mouth found on page 32 to give Salman his boofy pout. What did you think of those techniques? Pretty different, aren't they? See what you can do with this method for creating unusual, unpredictable organic shapes in your own creatures. Ultimately, enjoy the art of experimentation. You never know when you might be invited to contribute your findings to a stuffed toy book. (Can you say cliff-hanger?)

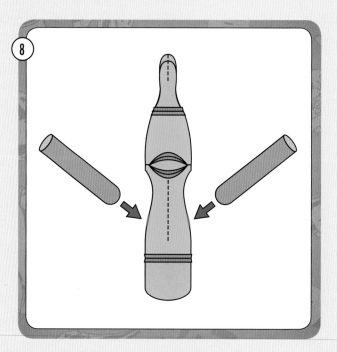

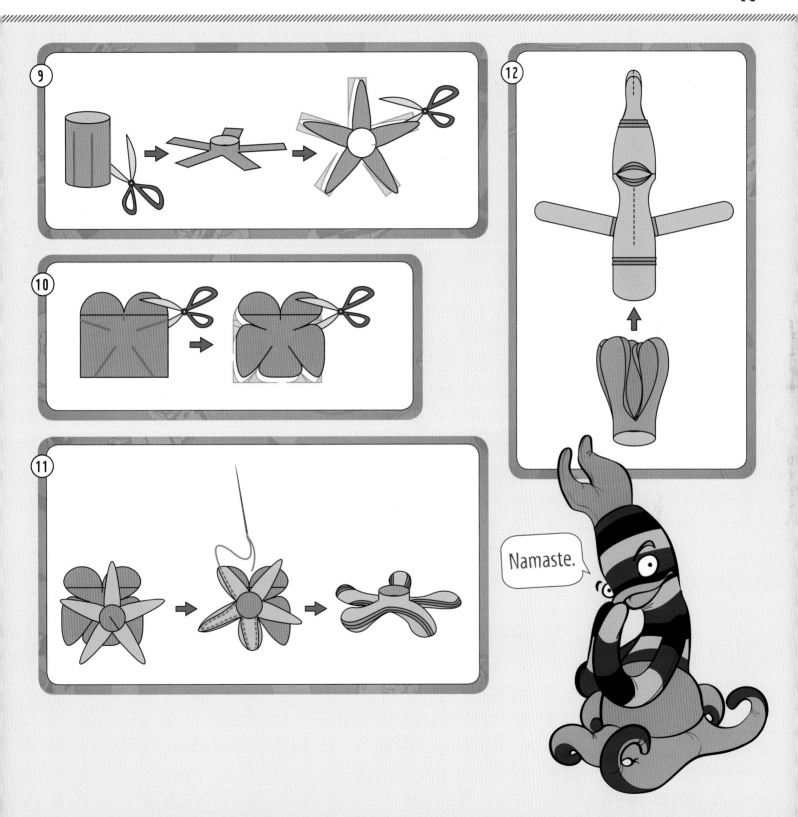

by John Murphy

STEVE

Steve Howard Manning is the kind of used-car salesman who can sell a car to another car. He once robbed a widow of her shawl and sold it back to her, convincing her she was cold in the middle of a blistering heat wave. It was awful. Steve crashed a convention full of strict vegetarians one day, and by the time he was done delivering his pitch, not only were they rabid meat eaters, but three of them had become cannibals.

You Will Need

- ✪ The Basic Creature Sewing Kit (page 9)
- ✪ 2 crew socks
- ✪ Supplies for Nice to T You eyes (page 32)

Cutting Out Your Parts

Check out **figure 1** to see how Steve ought to be cut. The first sock will largely be Steve's head and front legs. You'll only slice off a thick wedge of the foot and toe, which will become his back (and butt). The second sock will produce Steve's hindquarters (back legs and hips), his gut, tail, and ears. See **figure 2** for an inventory of each part you'll need.

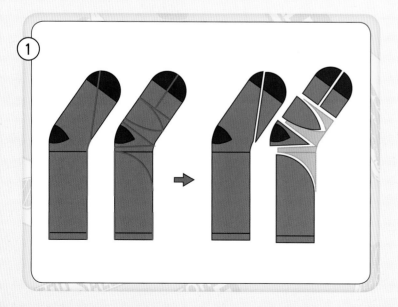

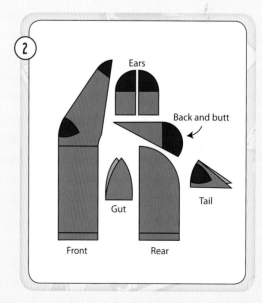

Sewing Steve

Take Steve's front and rear and turn them wrong side out. Flatten the front so that the heel faces upward, and flatten the rear the same way. See **figure 3** for a visual. Stitch leg shapes into the cuff ends of these body parts as shown in the diagram. Remember to notch and trim (see page 16) where necessary.

Flip both the front and rear pieces over just as you would a pancake, and make a vertical cut down the middle of only the top layer of each. Stop the cut within 1½ inches (3.8 cm) of the top of Steve's legs. These cuts will provide the place where you'll stitch in the gut **(figure 4)**.

See **figure 5**, and attach the gut to the slices you just made in Steve's front and rear using the vee method, found on page 22 of the Basics section. Attaching the back comes soon. It's a blast.

Before attaching the back, make and stuff the tail as shown in **figure 6**. Leave ½ inch (1.3 cm) of space unstuffed near the opening of the tail. There you go. Tails are wicked easy. Throughout this book you'll see loads of different tails. As you keep your scraps and odd cuttings, consider using them for tails of your own design. That's honestly what I do half the time.

So, to attach Steve's back, look at **figure 7**. Align the pointy end of the part you cut for Steve's back to the point at the top of his head. Make sure the right sides are touching. Stitch the two items together with a horizontal seam roughly 2 inches (5.1 cm) or so below the point. The lower you go, the wider the seam will be, which will widen the creature's neck and subsequently shorten the height of his head. None of this is necessarily bad, I just feel it's important that you know. If the points of these two items don't match, align the two pieces where their widths match nearest the points, and stitch there.

When you've made that seam, insert the tail inside Steve's rear, and align its open end with the point the curve at the back of his hindquarters **(figure 7)**. Pin the tail into place.

Figure 8 shows you how to bring the wide, rounded end of Steve's back over to meet the cut at the end of his rump. Pin the middle of the edge of Steve's butt to the point of the curve at the back of his hindquarters where you pinned the tail. In fact, you'll need to trap the tail between these two layers. Match and pin the edges on both sides about halfway up Steve's back toward his head.

The edges of Steve's head and back that you've thus far left unpinned should give you plenty of space to insert the ears, attaching them via the add-a-stub method (see page 26). Do that now **(figure 9)**.

With the ears now attached, it's time to match and pin all loose edges. Stitch from the point of one ear over to Steve's head, down his neck, across his back, around his butt, securing the tail as you go, and back up the other side till you reach the point of his other ear. Leave a 3-inch (7.6 cm) space unstitched along this seam for turning and stuffing **(figure 10)**.

And that's pretty much it. Turn Steve right side out carefully through the 3-inch (7.6 cm) opening. Stuff him thoroughly, and close up his stuffing hole using a ladder stitch. Follow the instructions for the Signature Stupid Sock Creature Mouth, found on page 32, to make lips from the heel in Steve's face.

To make Steve's eyes, follow the instructions for Nice to T You eyes found on page 32 of the Basics section. And that's that. Your version of Steve is ready to go separate some fools from their money. Enjoy using your new quadruped-making powers wherever you go.

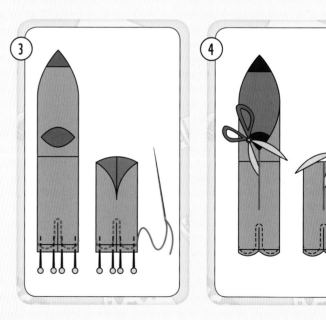

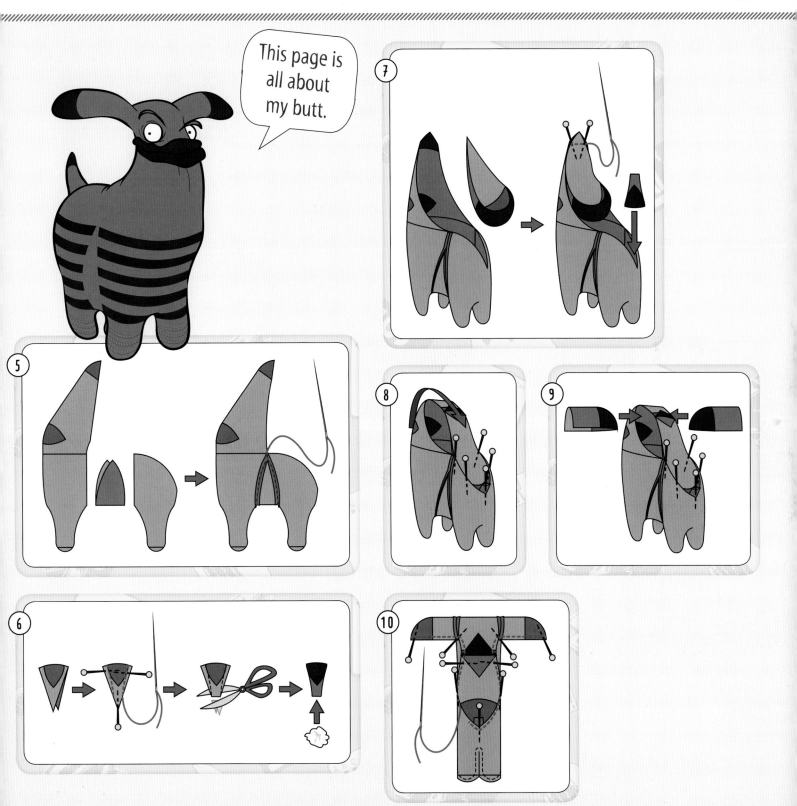

by Nate Little

ASHURBANIPAL

Don't let his burly physique fool you; Ashurbanipal is a Monster of Science—in archeology to be exact. He lives an adventurous, action-packed life searching for rare and mystical artifacts. He uses his dexterous hands and feet to help him safely navigate the many traps and dangers that lie within the ancient temples that he explores.

You Will Need

- ✪ The Basic Creature Sewing Kit (page 9)
- ✪ 2 matching toe socks
- ✪ Another sock you like, or a scrap and a heel from another project
- ✪ Buttons for eyes

Cutting Out Your Parts

Have a look at **figure 1** to see how to cut the toe socks, and what parts you'll need to harvest from your third sock. You'll save the majority of that third sock for another project.

The first toe sock will provide a two-toed arm, a three-toed leg, and Ashurbanipal's body. The second toe sock will provide the other arm and leg. The third sock will give up its heel for Ashurbanipal's mouth, and two triangular fragments will compose the spike in his head.

Look at **figure 2** for an overview of all the parts you should cut.

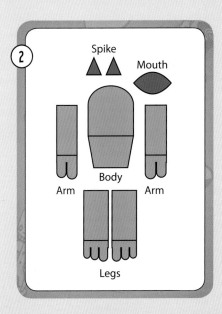

Sewing Ashurbanipal

Let's start with Ashurbanipal's body. All you need to do for this step is pin and stitch up the cut edges at his sides (**figure 3**).

Next, grab the heel you cut from your third sock and use its size to eyeball and cut a horizontal slit in Ashurbanipal's face. Chances are you're using a striped toe sock because most toe socks, in my experience, are striped, and you can use your stripes as guides for straight cuts. Make the slit approximately ½ inch (1.3 cm) shorter than the corner-to-corner width of the heel to provide for a seam allowance. When the cut is made, stitch the heel into place using the circumference method, as described on page 21 (**figure 4**).

To make Ashurbanipal's arms, use the two-toed sections you cut from the toe socks. Turn them wrong side out and stitch the open edges shut as shown in **figure 5**. Make a diagonal cut at the open edge of the arm to give Ashurbanipal's arms some slope at the shoulder.

Make Ashurbanipal's spike by aligning the two triangles you cut from the third sock, with right sides facing, and stitching two of the three sides (**figure 6**). You can cut a different shape for a spike if you want. You can even give him horns if you want. Assemble and attach them the very same way.

Snip and pry holes in Ashurbanipal's body for his arms and spike where you think those items ought to go, and use the circumference method to attach them (**figure 7**).

This next step is a tad particular but necessary to construct the feet the right way. Grab the three-toed parts you cut for Ashurbanipal's legs and feet. Lay one of them flat in front of you with the toes pointing towards you. You need to remove the top layer of tube material, leaving only the toes in tact.

At the largest toe, leave a triangular flap of tube intact at the toe's opening (**figure 8**). The triangle should be as equilateral as possible.

Each toe gets stitched to one side of the triangle. Since the largest toe has the triangle attached already, swing the middle toe around and match it up with the nearest free side of the triangle. Use a tight, secure overcast stitch (page 18) to join those edges together. You may need to stretch and finagle the edge of the toe to match the side of the triangle. Do the same with the little toe (**figure 9**). When you've got the toes stitched to the triangle, leave the side seam of the resulting leg unstitched for now.

Turn the feet and legs right side out. Use the add-a-stub method (page 26) to attach the legs to Ashurbanipal's body (**figure 10**). Now you can stitch up the side seams of the legs. Don't stitch the crotch shut yet.

Stuff Ashurbanipal thoroughly and close up his stuffing hole with a ladder stitch (**figure 11**).

Stitch buttons where you want Ashurbanipal's eyes, or follow any of the alternate methods found in the Basics section on page 30. And he's done. Let those bumbly digits navigate him to places the other creatures can only dream of going. It sure would stink if Ashurbanipal were smug about his ability to grasp things and perhaps balance on precarious terrain. I'm sure the other creatures are glad he's so uniquely endowed, because someone's got to uncover the secrets of the past. Maybe a team of Ferlin can help him dig, but who but Ashurbanipal with his capable hands and feet can grip stuff and show it off without dropping it?

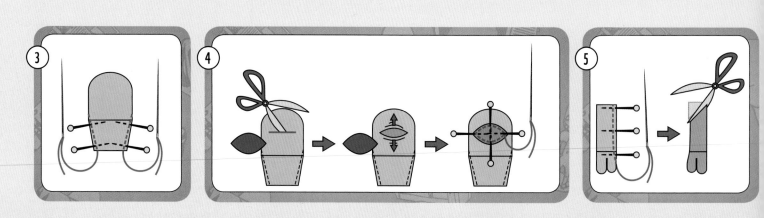

by John Murphy

ECTER PILFORY

It was a very strange day when Ecter Pilfory awoke to discover his pudding cups were all transformed into rusty cucumber sandwiches. To his shock, he discovered he'd read his instructional manual to the Midas Touch upside down and backward. Instead of endless wealth with the touch of a tiny claw, Ecter was doomed to a life of rusty little finger foods.

You Will Need

- ✪ The Basic Creature Sewing Kit (page 9)
- ✪ 1 crew sock
- ✪ 2 buttons for eyes

Cutting Out Your Parts

Observe the bright pink cut marks in **figure 1** and cut your sock accordingly. You'll make a head from the toe and part of the foot, so cut about half of the foot off the sock. Don't cut too much off for the head or you'll have too little left near the heel for Ecter's nubby little legs. The arms and ears will come from the tube of the sock, and the chunk in the middle with the heel will become Ecter's body and legs. You'll just need to snip out a 1-inch-wide (2.5 cm) wedge just above the heel to give Ecter's back a little contour. See **figure 2** for an overview of the parts you'll need.

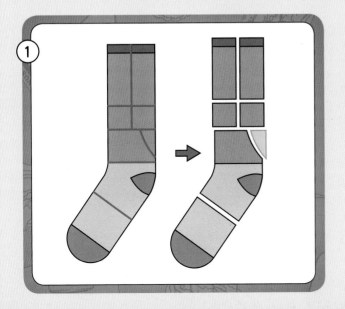

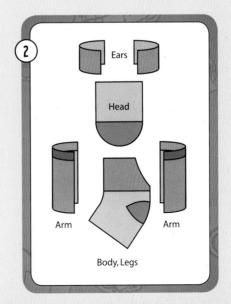

Sewing Ecter Pilfory

We'll start with the body. Stitch up the edge where you cut the wedge out for Ecter's back. Leave 1½ to 2 inches (3.8 to 5.1 cm) in the middle of this edge unstitched for stuffing him later (**figure 3**).

Pinch the feet edge closed horizontally and stitch a crotch, roughly 1½ inches (3.8 cm) deep and perhaps ½ inch (1.3 cm) wide (figure 4). Be careful not to stitch into the heel of your sock or your Ecter will lean too far forward when he's stitched and stuffed. He'll look like he's smelling the floor or something. This might make any nearby Snarfles mad if they think he's eating their crumbs and shiny things. Imagine that fight. Teeth and rusty finger food in a nasty whirlwind. I don't think there's a spray that can lift those stains. I guess you could presoak. But never mind. The point is to avoid disaster by making Ecter's crotch just the right dimension.

Once disaster is averted, pinch Ecter's feet shut, as shown in **figure 4**, and stitch them closed. This will give the feet some dimension, and will keep him from falling over (as much) when he sits.

Alright. Onward to Ecter's head. This one might require a video tutorial later 'cause it took me ages to come up with diagrams for this reasonably easy step. Grab the severed toe part you cut for Ecter's head and turn it wrong side out. In the very same way someone laments over his or her figure and grabs at a love handle, pinch a fold roundabout where the toe begins (**figure 5**). If your sock's toe is a different color from the rest of the sock, then this step should be simple. If not, then just pick a place down toward the toe and pinch a love handle.

Place pins in the love handle to mark where you want Ecter's teeth to go, or rather, the spaces between Ecter's teeth. I recommend no more than four to five pins depending on the width of your sock. The sock I used for Ecter yielded six teeth, but given that each one needed a seam allowance, it's best not to expect that number of teeth from every sock. Stitch around the pins on the love handle. Remove the pins, and trim and notch the spaces where you inserted them (**figure 6**).

Use the add-a-stub attachment method, found on page 26 of the Basics section, to graft Ecter's ears onto his head. When that's done, stitch a rounded edge at the top of one ear, stitch down the ear across the top of the head, then finish the

second ear the way you did the first (**figure 7**). Notch the space between the ears and trim the curved edges.

Snip and pry a hole in the bottom of Ecter's head to fit his neck opening. Turn the head right side out via this hole. Keep Ecter's body wrong side out, and shove the head down his neck, matching the neck opening with the hole in the bottom of the head. Make sure that Ecter's teeth are oriented toward the front of his body. Follow the circumference method (page 21) to stitch the head and body together (**figure 8**). Turn Ecter right side out through the hole in his back, and stuff him. Use a ladder stitch to close up his stuffing hole.

Follow the Jabby Hands instructions on page 27 to make Ecter's arms. Stuff them, and ladder stitch them to Ecter's sides wherever you think arms ought to go. And there you have it.

Use buttons for Ecter's eyes, or choose from the various eye options starting on page 30 of the Basics section. Ecter is now finished and ready to practice his cursed perversion of alchemy on the world around him.

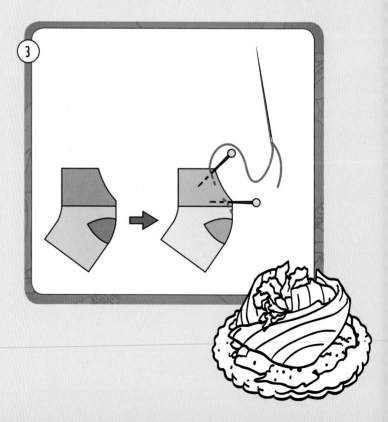

See? Easy as rusty pie.

by Kittypinkstars

RAINBOW DRIBBLE

Rainbow Dribble is a seven-foot-tall giant who likes to drink from a rainbow-colored waterfall. He shows concern for whomever he finds near his home and makes friends quickly. Most are startled when they meet Rainbow Dribble (RBD for short), but he puts people at ease right away.

You Will Need

- ✪ The Basic Creature Sewing Kit (page 9)
- ✪ 2 pairs of toe socks in different colors
- ✪ 1 additional toe sock, a different color if available
- ✪ 3 wire coat hangers
- ✪ Tape
- ✪ 2 child-safe doll eyes

Cutting Out Your Parts

The cuts for RBD are pretty simple. **Figure 1** shows which cuts to make and where. Make sure you look at **figure 2** for an overview of all the parts your socks ought to yield for your creature. There are a good number of them.

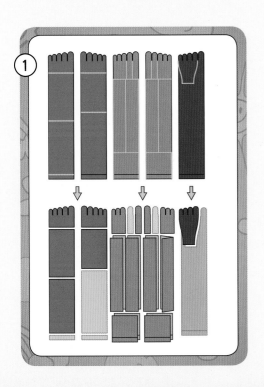

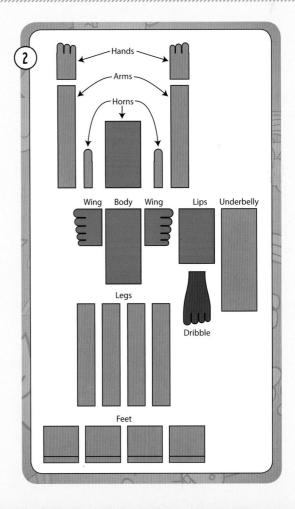

Sewing Rainbow Dribble

We'll start with something simple. Kittypinkstars allows you to employ your imagination right off the bat by leaving the shape of RBD's large middle horn up to you. Grab the parts you cut for that horn, and stitch the horn shape that pleases you best (**figure 3**). Trim the excess fabric, and turn the horn right side out. Stuff it and set it aside.

Next, we'll take care of several simple things all at once. The arms, the hands, and the smaller horns all need to be stitched closed. Turn each of those items wrong side out. In the case of the arms, you'll need to fold each strip vertically in half with the right sides facing. Stitch the cut edges of each item shut as shown in **figure 4**. When you've done that, stuff them.

You'll proceed to attach the hands to the ends of the arms. Both items are stuffed, and you'll likely find that, if you're following these instructions to the letter, the opening to the hand is wider than the opening of the arms. In any case, you need to shove the end of the arm into the opening of the hand. Tuck the edge of the hand under to hide its raw edge, and baste a running stitch around the edge. Cinch the hand shut around the arm, and use ladder stitches or overcast stitches to anchor the hand to the arm. Do the same to the other hand and arm. See **figure 5** for clarification.

Here comes a fun part. It's time to prepare some wire to go inside your arms. Cut apart one of your coat hangers. Make

sure it's twice as long as one of RDB's arms, plus 6 or so inches (15.2 cm) longer. In fact, do this three times since you'll need two additional lengths of wire down the road when it's time to make your creatures' legs. Prepare the cut ends of your wire by bending ½ inch (1.3 cm) of the end tightly backward and binding it with sturdy tape (**figure 6**). This will prevent the cut end of your wire from poking through the arm fabric.

Bend the wire gently in half and insert its bound ends into the arms all the way to the hands. You'll have to kind of creep the ends of the wire past all the stuffing (**figure 7**). It might be a tad weird, but you'll figure it out.

Here comes a part that's easier than it looks. Grab the part you cut for RBD's body and turn it wrong side out. Arrange your small horns, arms, and the big horn as shown in **figure 8**. Shove them all up inside the body and arrange their open ends with the edge of the body. It might take some manipulating and futzing to get everything to lie side by side in a neat little row.

Figure 9 shows you how to pin and stitch the ends of the arms and horns to the edge of RBD's body. You'll use what amounts to the circumference method (see page 21). Work tight backstitches (see page 18) or overcast stitches. Leave plenty of seam allowance. This part is best done by hand since it's a bit intricate and involves coat-hanger wire, which will destroy a sewing machine needle.

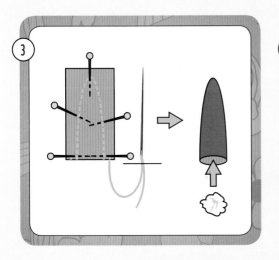

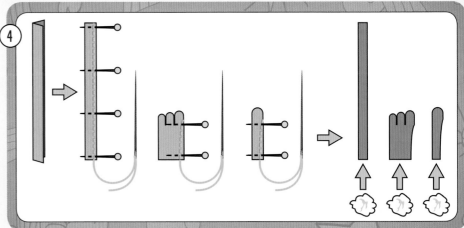

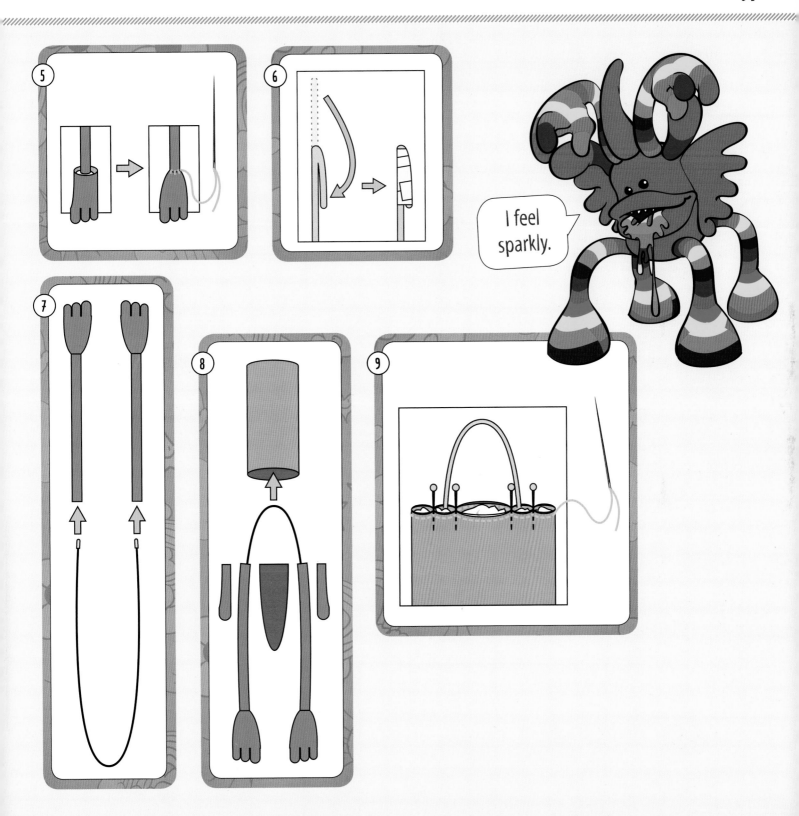

Alright. Time for the feet. Grab the four squares of cuff and tube you cut for the feet and fold them vertically in half with right sides touching. Stitch only the rib of this foot. When that's done, open up the foot kind of like a vampire might flap his cape open while shouting, "BLAAH!" The edges will form an arc. Fold the flat edge at the bottom of the arc upward to meet the point at the top of the arc. It's best to stitch the middle point of the flat edge to that point and hand stitch down the edges until you reach the fold, as shown in **figure 10**. When you're done, trim the corners of the flat edge you've turned up.

When you turn your foot right side out again it should look similar to what you see in **figure 11**. Stuff the feet at this time. The legs of your creature are cut from parts identical to the arms. Reference figure 4 again to see how they should be turned and stitched. When you've done that, stuff all four legs.

In the very same way the hands were attached to the arms, attach the feet to the legs. See **figure 12** for an image.

Here's where things start to get interesting, and you begin to see your creature come together. Grab the armed, horned body of your RBD and attach its child-safe eyes where you think they

ought to go. Instructions for attaching child-safe eyes can be found in the Nice to T You instructions on page 32. Stuff the body thoroughly, and then snip some tiny openings where you think the legs ought to go, roughly 1 inch (2.5 cm) away from the bottom edge **(figure 13)**. You want these openings just wide enough to usher the coat-hanger wire supports through.

So, since you've cut wire already to a suitable length (back when you were making arms), grab those two lengths of wire. Slide them through the slits you made in RBD's body so that they intersect in the middle **(figure 14)**. When the exact middles of those wires have intersected, bind them with sturdy tape as shown in **figure 15** to hold them into place.

Alright. Time to slide the legs on. The very same way you managed to scoot the arms onto their wire supports, slide the legs onto their wires at the base of the body. See **figure 16** if any of this is confusing. Tuck the open edges of the legs under to hide the raw edge, and stitch the legs to the slits in the body using a ladder stitch. Pack a little extra stuffing into the opening of the legs to fill them out if necessary.

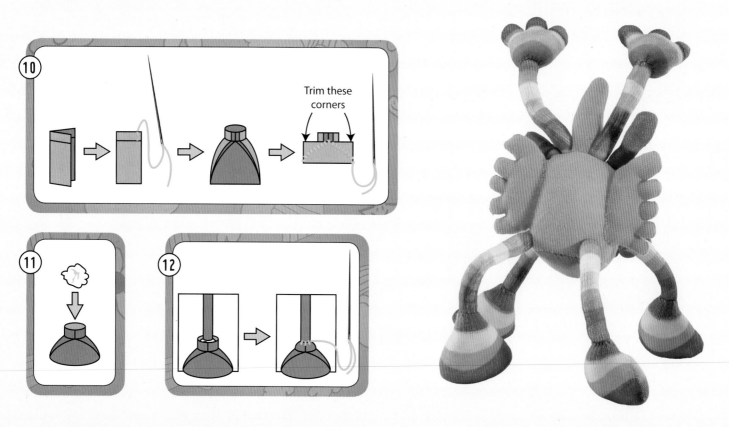

(10)

Trim these corners

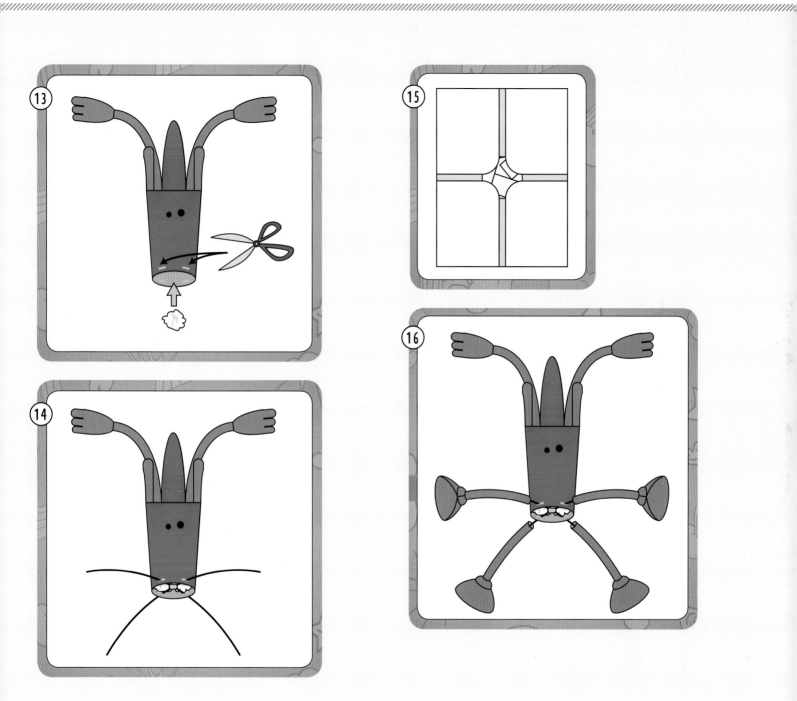

So, it's time to close up your creature's body. Grab the piece of fabric you cut for RBD's underbelly. Tuck the ends of it up inside the body till its middle is flat against all the stuffing and hides the wires. Tuck the edge of the body inside itself to hide the raw edge. Use overcast or ladder stitches to secure the tucked edge of the body to the underbelly, as shown in **figure 17**.

Turn your attention now to RBD's dribble. Find the piece of the toe sock you cut for that part and turn it wrong side out. Stitch up the open edges as shown in **figure 18** and stuff it very lightly. You want it to stay pretty much flat, but it ought to have a little volume.

Grab the piece of tube you cut for RBD's lips and turn it wrong side out. Insert the dribble as shown in **figure 19**, and match its open edge with an end of the tube segment.

See **figure 20** and follow the Tiptoe through the Tube Lips instructions, found on page 34 of the Basics section, to turn that tube segment and dribble into a pair of boofy, drooling lips.

You're nearly done—and likely can predict what comes next. **Figure 21** indicates that it's time to stuff the wings. Do that. Stuff them pretty thoroughly, and attach them to RBD's body using a ladder stitch, as shown in **figure 22**, wherever you think they ought to go.

I'll bet by now you've learned an awful lot about how to attach parts to a creature. This project should give you ideas for sprucing up existing creatures or adding steps to other projects. Have a blast!

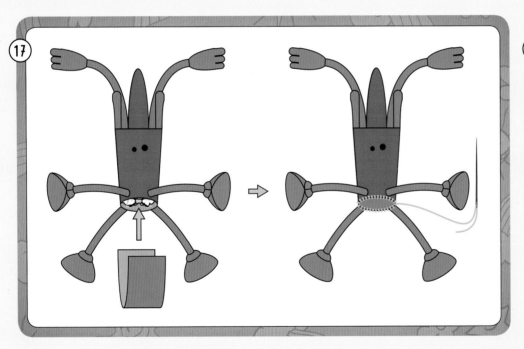

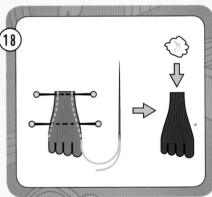

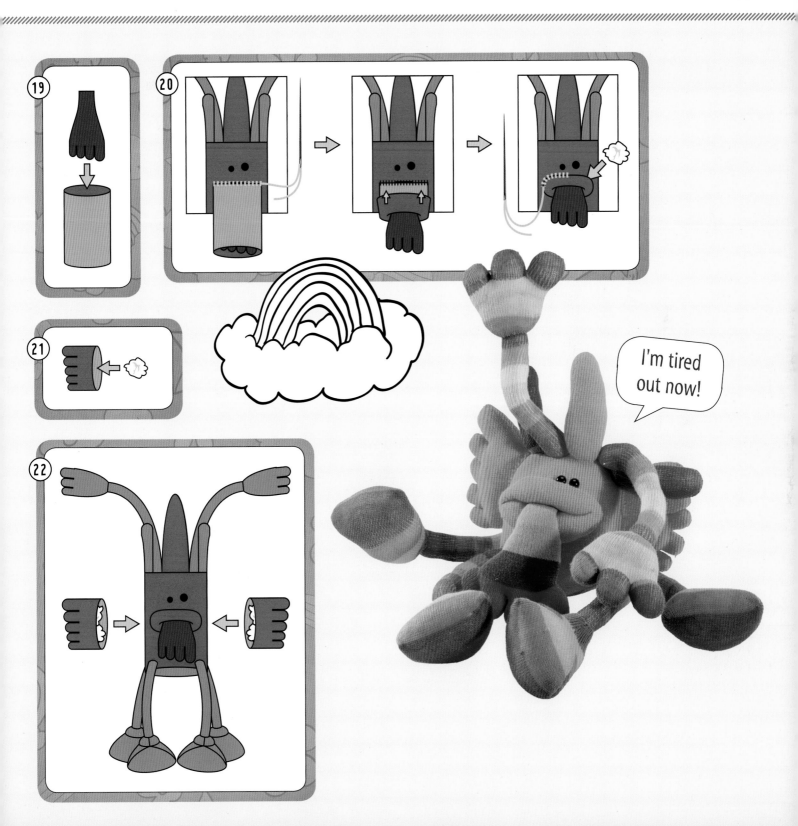

I'm tired out now!

by Ed Saul

DESDEMONA

Desdemonas don't have mouths or noses; they eat and breathe pure story, and they grow attached to the world's storytellers. Desdemonas can be found on library bookshelves, empty train seats, or even under the bed.

You Will Need

- ✪ The Basic Creature Sewing Kit (page 9)
- ✪ 1 plain crew sock
- ✪ 1 vivid or patterned knee sock
- ✪ 1 button for her eye

Cutting Out Your Parts

Observe the bright blue cut marks in **figure 1** to see how you should destroy your socks for this project. You'll see in **figure 2** the designated purpose for the pieces you cut from the two socks.

The plain crew sock will be irreversibly disfigured to become Desdemona's body, and the knee sock will be mercilessly hacked apart to provide Desdemona's face, tentacles, and fins. Desdemona's face is essentially an oval, cut approximately ½ inch (1.3 cm) wider and taller than the heel you removed from her body sock. She's going to be gorgeous—I guarantee it.

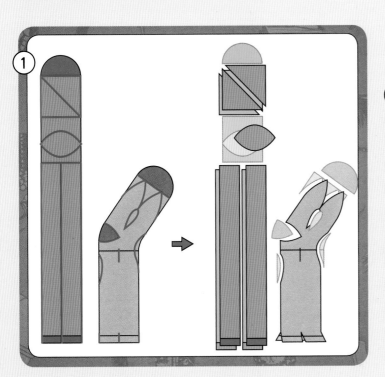

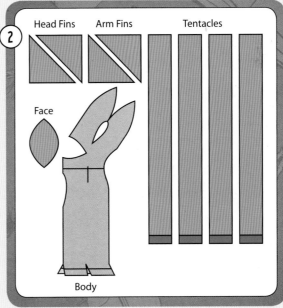

Sewing Desdemona

We'll start by converting all those slashes and gouges in Desdemona's body into the curves and contours of her delicate, slender, mollusk-like form. Have a look at **figure 3** for details. With Desdemona's body on her side, stitch the front- and back-neck curves. Leave a 2-inch (5.1 cm) space in the back-neck curve unstitched for turning and stuffing. Turn Desdemona face up, and stitch the side-neck curves and the side contours of her head, which create squidlike outcroppings. Make sure to notch and trim as necessary (see page 16).

To finish off Desdemona's head, grab the two triangles you cut for her head fins. Fold them in half with the right side out. Insert the triangles, folded side down, into Desdemona's head. Use the vee method, found on page 22 of the Basics section, to attach the fins to the front and back curves of her head. Pull the attached fins out of Desdemona's head. Align your seams and pin. Stitch from the corner of one fin, across the top of her head, and straight to the corner of the second fin **(figure 4)**. Notch and trim where necessary.

See **figure 5** to make Desdemona's arm fins. Fold the remaining two triangles as shown, and stitch accordingly. Trim the seam allowance at the corner near the fold. Turn the fins right side out.

Attach the fins to Desdemona's body using the circumference method, found on page 21 of the Basics section **(figure 6)**. Remember to snip and pry as instructed; do not attack her like you're a frat boy and she's a keg. She is a delicate, graceful swimmer in the sparkling oceans of our dreams—she is not a sinking dirigible, spewing flames along with the screams of terrified passengers as hungry sharks lurk and circle in wait. But that might be cool to watch.

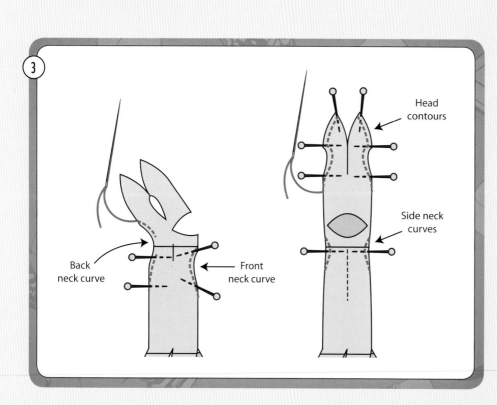

3

Head contours

Side neck curves

Back neck curve

Front neck curve

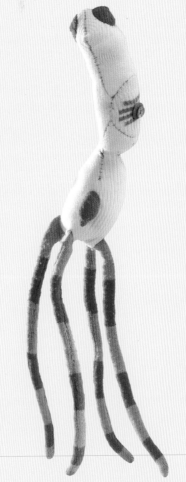

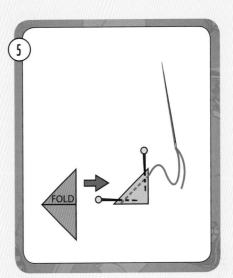

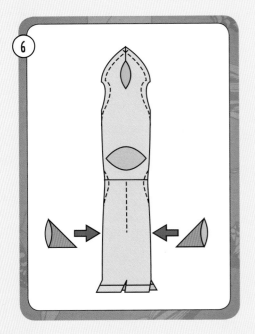

I have no knees!

When her fins are attached, pull them out from her body and lay Desdemona face up. It's time to attach her face. You'll need to align the face oval vertically to Desdemona's horizontal mouth. This will involve cajoling the dimensions of her mouth opening to accommodate the shape of the face. Once that's done, pin it into place and attach the face using the circumference method. See **figure 7** for a visual.

Turn your attention to the long strips of knee-sock tube you cut for Desdemona's lovely tentacles. Grab a strip and fold it in half vertically, with the wrong side out. Pin and stitch straight down the long edge, and curve your seam to make a point at the end of the tentacle. Trim the seam allowance at the tentacle's point, turn it right side out, and stuff it lightly. Follow these instructions three more times to make the other tentacles **(figure 8)**.

Keep Desdemona's body inside out and insert the open edges of her tentacles into the slits you made in the cuff of her body. Use the slit method (see page 22) to stitch the tentacles into place **(figure 9)**.

When all four tentacles are attached, stuff them down into Desdemona's inside-out body. Close up the cuff by making an X out of the round opening, and overcast stitch (see page 18) it shut. Observe **figure 10** to see approximately what it should look like.

Once Desdemona's bottom is sewn shut (ouch!), turn her right side out through the opening you left at the back of her neck. Stuff her as firmly as you like, remembering she is an elegant, silky, willowy, sylphlike gem of the deep, deep fathoms and should not wind up lumpy like a pig. Use a ladder stitch, as instructed on page 18 of the Basics section, to shut her stuffing hole.

Stitch a button to the middle of her face, or use any of the eye options found on page 30. And with a splash, Desdemona is finished. Chances are, if you actually stuck your Desdemona in the water, she'd just become soggy since she's made of socks and fiberfill, and we don't recommend that. But enjoy her alien gracefulness anytime you're sick of looking at ugly things.

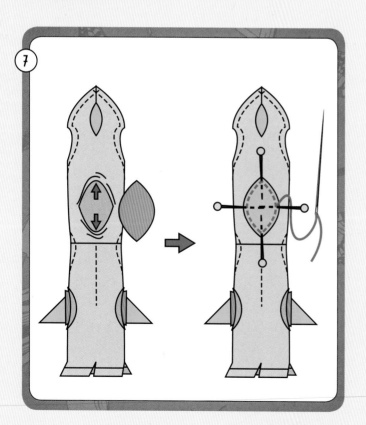

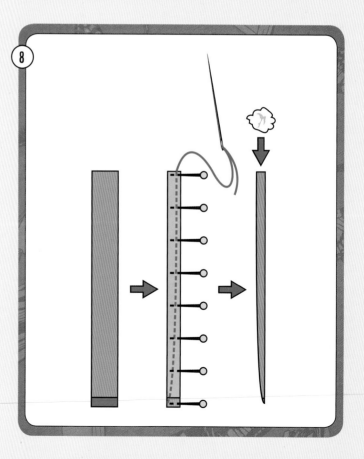

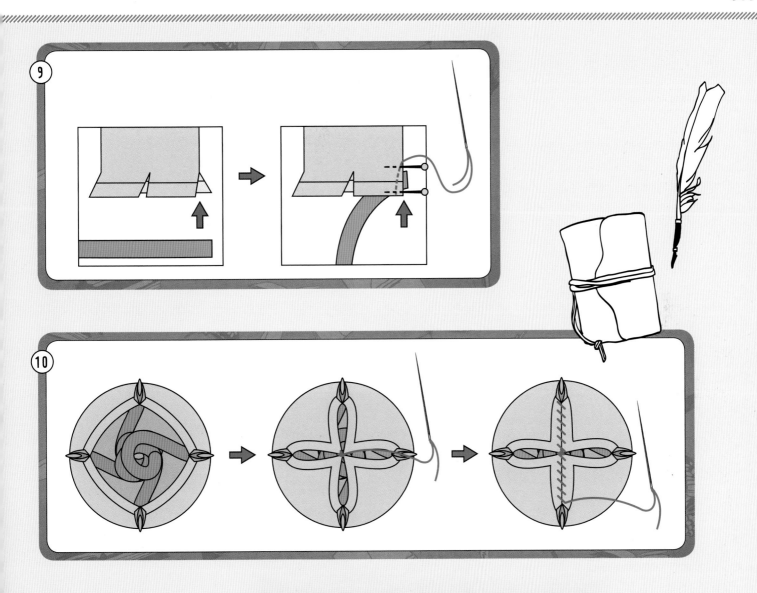

Few people can get away with haphazard, rag doll stitchery, but Ed does it well. He hand stitches everything and doesn't let the wonky results stop him! I like his work because it shows that anyone with an active imagination can and should try his or her hand at making a sock monster.

by Kelly McCaffrey

QUEEGSLY

Queegsly likes to perch in high places, especially near burger joints where he regularly steals pickles from unsuspecting sandwiches. Most of his species have two toes and a slightly prehensile tail. The rare polydactyl, Queegsly has an extra, vestigial toe.

You Will Need

- ✪ The Basic Creature Sewing Kit (page 9)
- ✪ 2 crew socks
- ✪ 2 pipe cleaners (optional)
- ✪ Buttons for eyes

Cutting Out Your Parts

See the blue cut marks in **figure 1** to see how your socks should be cut and portioned. The first sock will provide Queegsly's feet, his body, and one of his wings. The second sock will provide the other wing, his tail, his base, his eye stalks, and his back. See **figure 2** to see what parts you should have cut and the purpose each will serve in this creature.

A couple more cuts are required before you start to sew. Take Queegsly's body and lay it heel side down. Make a vertical slice down the middle of the heel-less side to make a flat rectangular piece **(figure 3)**. Take the part you cut for Queegsly's base and round its corners off **(figure 4)**.

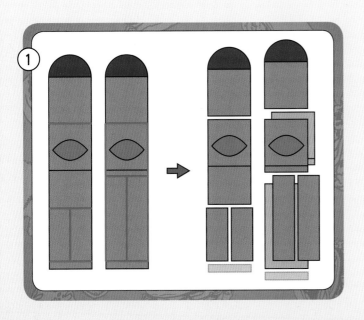

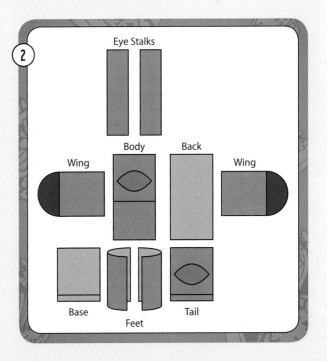

Sewing Queegsly

Lay Queegsly's body flat with the right side up. With right sides together, align one vertical edge of his back to a corresponding short edge on one side of the body. Pin and stitch those edges together. Align the other vertical edge with the side of the body opposite the seam you just made. Pin and stitch those edges, but leave a 2-inch (5.1 cm) space unstitched along that seam for turning and stuffing later (**figure 5**).

Grab the parts you cut for Queegsly's feet and fold them in half vertically with the wrong side out. Pin the edges and stitch a long, two-toed foot into the shape as shown in **figure 6**. Notch and trim (see page 16) the seam allowances around the foot and turn it right side out. Stuff the foot thoroughly, but leave ½ inch (1.3 cm) of space unstuffed at the opening.

Take the part you cut for Queegsly's tail and fold it in half as shown in **figure 7**. Stitch a spiky tail shape—or what have you—leaving one end open for turning and stuffing. Trim and notch the seam allowances as necessary, and turn the tail right side out. Stuff the tail thoroughly, leaving ½ inch (1.3 cm) of space unstuffed at the opening.

When the feet and tail are stitched and stuffed, insert them into Queegsly's body through the bottom opening. Pin these parts where you think they ought to go. Kelly designed Queegsly to have his feet point out to the sides, but you can place them wherever you'd like. Tails typically belong in the middle of a creature's butt if one hopes to convey that it is a tail at all (**figure 8**).

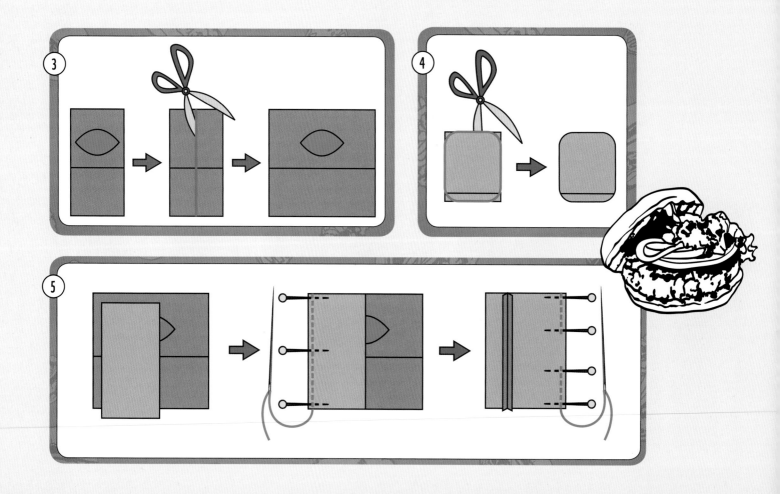

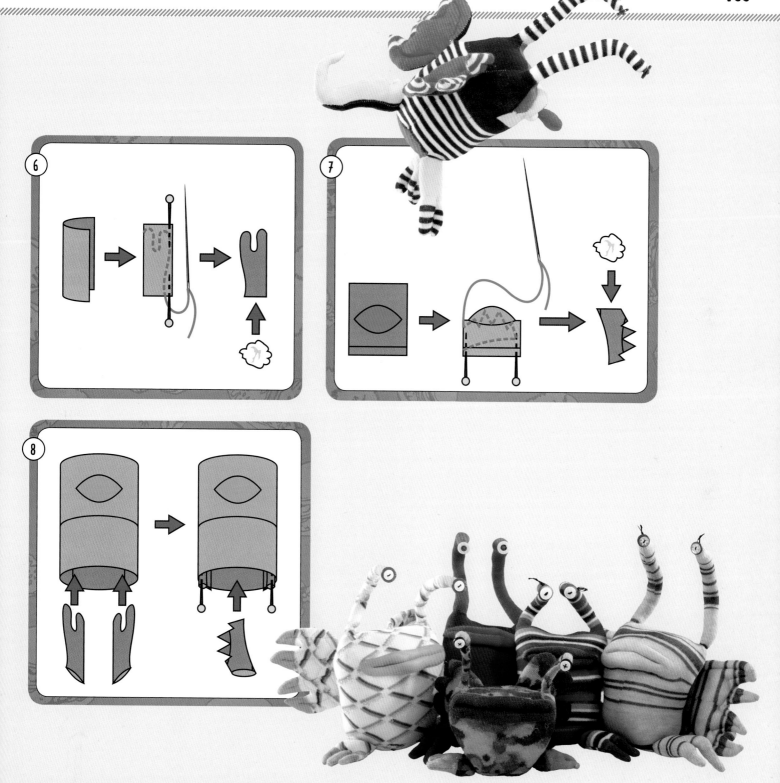

After securing those parts with pins, take the rounded base piece you cut and align it with the bottom edge of Queegsly's body. It's okay to gently stretch Queegsly's base in case it's a tad small to fit the opening. In any case, you must stitch the base to the body, securing the open ends of the feet and tail in the seam **(figure 9)**. This is a combination of the circumference and slit methods (pages 21 and 22). I love this line of work. You can twist the rules if you so wish.

To make Queegsly's wings, grab the socks' toe sections you cut for Queegsly's wings. Turn them wrong side out and stitch a wing shape of your liking. Notch and trim the seam allowances as necessary and turn the wings right side out. Stuff the wings lightly and flatten the stuffing to distribute it evenly throughout the wings. Topstitch a linear pattern in the wings to add detail and stability to these parts. It's really pretty attractive **(figure 10)**.

Snip and pry some small slits into Queegsly's back where you think the wings ought to go. Insert the wings, "feathers" first, into those slits and attach them using the slit method **(figure 11)**. Make these attachments especially strong so that Queegsly can flap his wings with gusto.

Alright. Onward to the eye stalks. Grab the long strips you cut for those stalks and attach them to the top edge of Queegsly's body using the add-a-stub (page 26) method **(figure 12)**. Pull the eye stalks out of Queegsly's body and align their vertical edges and the edges at the top of the head. Pin and stitch these edges as shown in figure 12. These eye stalks will be pretty narrow, so use only what seam allowance is necessary. Go for ⅛ to ³⁄₁₆ inch (.3 to .5 cm), but no less.

Trim and notch the seam allowances at the eye stalks as necessary and turn Queegsly right side out. Pull wings and feet through the unstitched part of his back seam. Be gentle about this process.

You'll need to use a stuffing tool such as the point turner, a chopstick, or a crochet hook from your Basic Creature Sewing Kit to turn the eye stalks right side out. In any case, you'll need to go slowly and carefully to turn them right side out. When you've done that, now's the time to insert pipe cleaners into the stalks if you so desire. Cut your pipe cleaners to size, or twist extra length onto them if necessary. You'll have to stuff very gently and very slowly around the eye stalks by inserting tiny bits of stuffing at a time.

Stuff the remainder of Queegsly's body as normal. Close up his stuffing hole with a ladder stitch. Follow the instructions for the Signature Stupid Sock Creature Mouth (page 32) to make Queegsly's mouth out of the heel in his body. Attach button eyes to the ends of Queegsly's eye stalks and bend them to affect the facial expression you desire.

Wasn't that insightful? I'm guessing by now your creature is insisting you queue up at a burger joint for some limp, tasty pickle slices. I hope you enjoy the quilting and eye stalk techniques. Apply them liberally to thousands of bizarre new creatures.

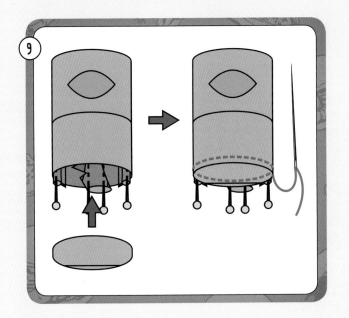

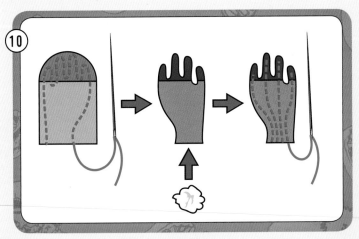

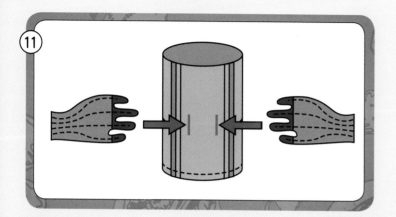

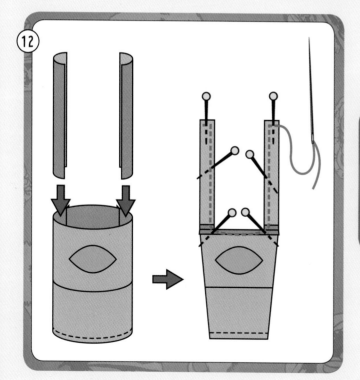

This project will appeal to anyone with an eye for detail and intricate work. Queegsly features quilted body parts and has a very dynamic anatomy. The way Kelly attaches body parts using structural seams and the slit method should give you plenty of ideas for your own original work. Pay special attention to Queegsly's eye stalks. Use pipe cleaners to bend and pose them!

by Jennifer Brett

BOB

Bob, the one-finned, two-horned monster, evolved in a library from abandoned items in the lost-and-found bin. He awoke to discover he was alone and unique, and he began reading everything he could find to discover his life's purpose—or at least what species he is.

You Will Need

- ✪ The Basic Creature Sewing Kit (page 9)
- ✪ 1 crew sock with a heel
- ✪ 1 toe sock of any color or pattern you want
- ✪ 2 buttons for eyes

Cutting Out Your Parts

Observe the bright blue cut marks in **figure 1** and cut your socks accordingly. The crew sock will become Bob's head and body, and it only needs the toe removed. The toe sock will provide Bob's fin, ears, and arms. Because Bob is such a simple design, consider using remnants from other projects to provide his basic features, or even something extra. Whatever you decide, see **figure 2** for a breakdown of the parts you'll need.

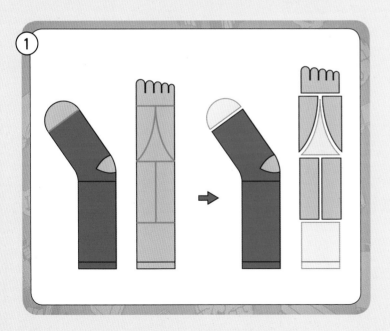

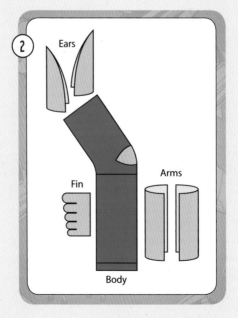

Sewing Bob

Turn Bob's body wrong side out. Arrange it flat with the heel facing upward. Stitch two stubby legs toward the cuff of the sock. Make the legs as long as you want, bearing in mind the sock has to accommodate two arms and a fin **(figure 3)**. Separate the legs by cutting between the seams, and trim and notch where necessary (see page 16).

Keep Bob's body wrong side out, and insert the ears' tips first into Bob's head **(figure 4)**. Match the straight edges of the ears with the straight edge of Bob's head, and use the add-a-stub attachment method (see page 26) to stitch them on.

Pull the ears out of Bob's head and flatten them. Stitch the open edges of both ears, leaving 1 inch (2.5 cm) of each ear toward the head unstitched. This will be the stuffing access **(figure 5)**.

Grab the parts you cut for Bob's arms. Fold them in half vertically with the wrong side out. Stitch a rounded seam at one of the short edges, and stitch straight up the long edge. Leave the other short edge open for turning and attaching **(figure 6)**. Repeat these steps for the second arm.

Turn the arms right side out. Follow the circumference method instructions on page 21 to attach Bob's arms to his body **(figure 7)**. Please, please, and 100 times please, remember to snip and pry the holes in Bob's body where you intend to attach the arms. If you hack open a hole, you run the risk of making that hole too big.

When the arms are attached and secure, pull them out of Bob's body the same way you did his ears. Cut a vertical slit down Bob's back that's ½ inch (1.3 cm) shorter than the length of his fin **(figure 8)**.

Lightly stuff Bob's fin, and insert it, curved edge first, into the slit on his back. Use the slit method, found on page 22 of the Basics section, to close Bob up in the back, clamping the fin into place as you go **(figure 9)**.

To finish Bob, turn him right side out through the hole you left in his head. Stuff Bob through that hole, imagining that each blob of stuffing is the embodiment of enlightenment. Fill your Bob with a sense of purpose and a drive to grow in knowledge. Give him meaning, intent, and a personality that isn't annoying or overly philosophical, because people who think too much

usually get on everyone's nerves. Then they numb their butts for six hours straight writing poetry at a coffee shop where everyone can see them in their fingerless gloves. Ultimately, have a blast with Bob. Expand upon him, evolve him, and perpetuate him. And tell him, no matter how brooding and beatnik-like it makes him look, to avoid smoking at all costs, especially if he has a synthetic fiber content.

Gosh. I almost forgot. Follow the Signature Stupid Sock Creature Mouth instructions on page 32 to give Bob his existential pout of longing. Use buttons for eyes, or choose from the array of eye suggestions in the Basics section (see page 30).

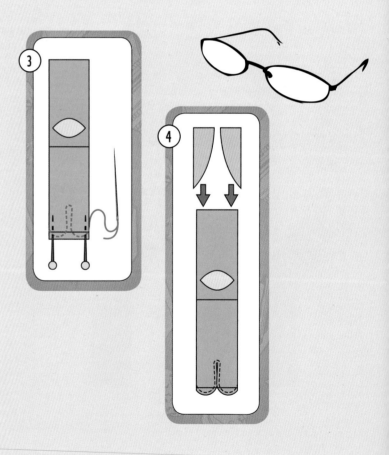

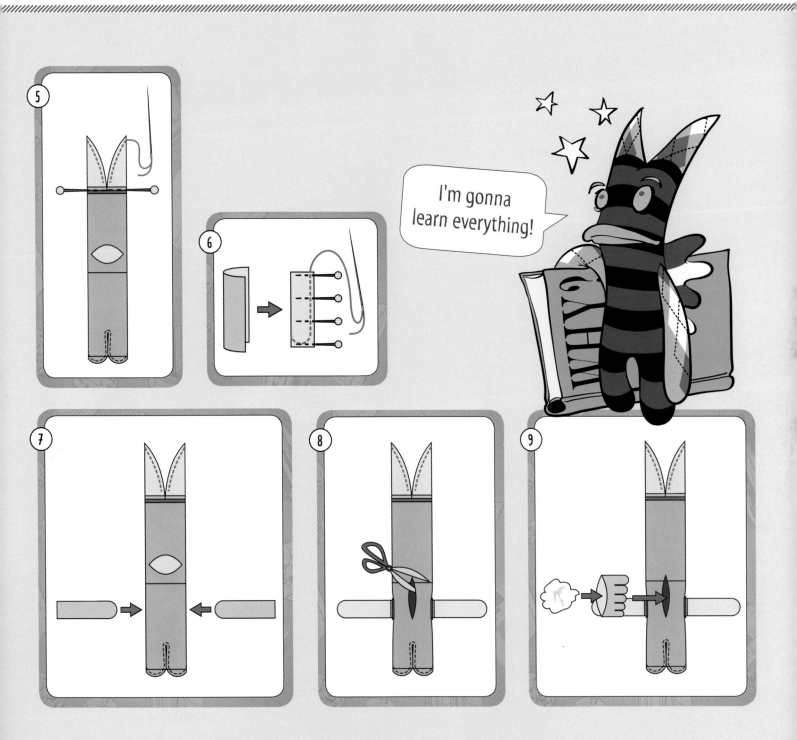

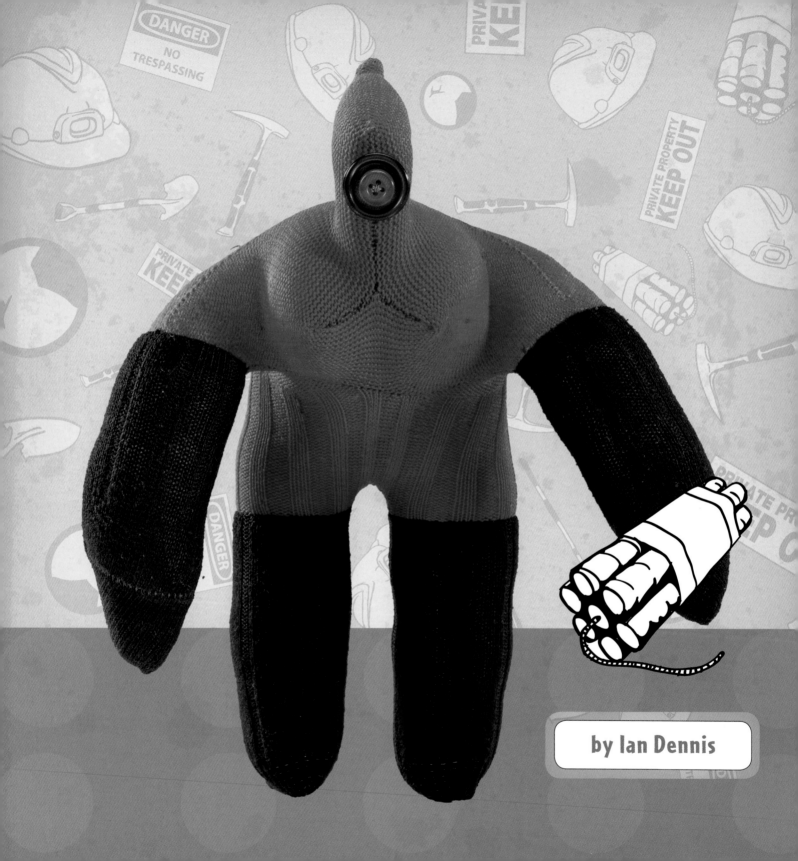

by Ian Dennis

FERLIN

Ferlins are small, semi-amphibious burrowing cyclopes. Though timid and solitary by nature, they are nonetheless regarded as pests, as their riverbank burrows have a tendency to collapse during heavy rains, contributing to erosion and creating the occasional sinkhole.

You Will Need

- ✪ The Basic Creature Sewing Kit (page 9)
- ✪ 2 contrasting crew socks (incidentally, you can get Ferlin from 1 crew sock, but we're going to mix and match parts from 2 different ones)
- ✪ Buttons for one eye (try layering a small one atop a large one for some added expression)

Cutting Out Your Parts

Observe the yellow cut marks in **figure 1**. You'll make arms from the toe and legs from the tube. The rest of the sock will be Ferlin's body. Cut a vertical slit through the heel (in the top layer) about as long as the heel is wide. Don't cut through the back layer of the sock, because that would be tragic.

See **figure 2** for the very easily remembered configuration of parts Ferlin will need to be complete.

Turn Ferlin's body to the side and lay it flat. Make a diagonal cut, about 1 inch (2.5 cm), into Ferlin's back near his head. See **figure 3** for clarification. That completes all the cutting you'll need to do to Ferlin's parts.

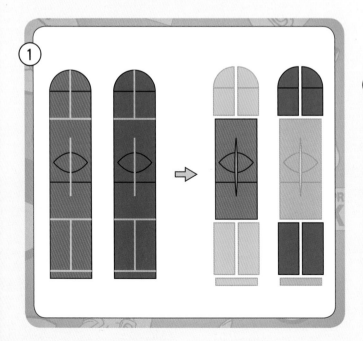

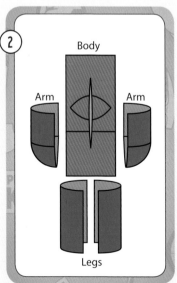

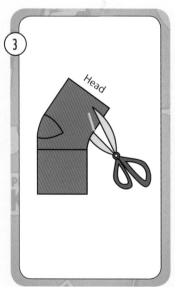

Sewing Ferlin

Turn the body wrong side out, and arrange it heel side up. Attach the legs to Ferlin's body using the add-a-stub method found on page 26 of the Basics section (**figure 4**).

The next step is what makes this project so unique. The cut you made through the heel in figure 1 will need to be squashed and manipulated to go horizontally. See **figure 5**. When you manipulate the slit, it will cause the opening at the top of the body to lean forward, and you'll notice the little cut created in figure 3 will pop up in the back. All of these steps give Ferlin his unique shape and appearance.

Use the add-a-stub method again to attach Ferlin's arms into this slit as shown in **figure 6**. When you've done that, turn Ferlin to the side and stitch the cut in the back of his head as shown in **figure 7**.

To finish stitching Ferlin, lay him flat on his back. You'll need to close up his face by squashing the edges of the opening inward to make an upside-down Y. Use a tight overcast stitch to close up this feature. Refer to **figure 8** if any of that sounds weird.

Now you need to turn Ferlin right side out and stuff him thoroughly. Close up his stuffing hole using a ladder stitch. Add Ferlin's eye using the buttons you selected or consider a different eye solution as suggested on page 30 of the Basics section.

This project is probably one of the simpler ones in the book, but it's also one of the most sculptural. I hope you'll apply these techniques to something equally as strange and original as Ferlin.

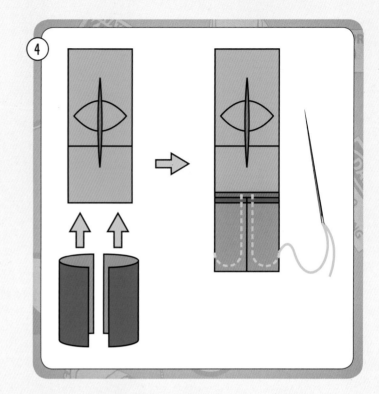

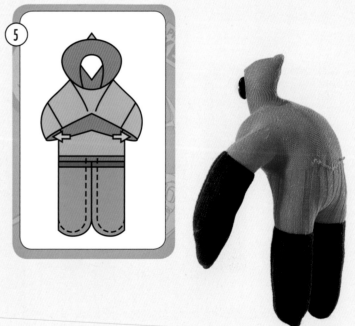

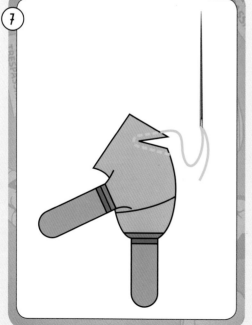

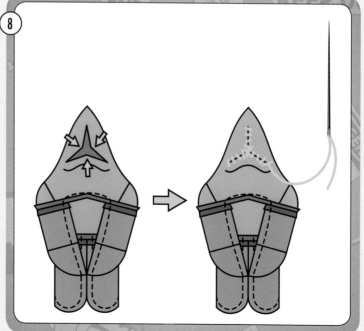

by John Murphy

MORV & GOPER

Every Wednesday, Morv goes down to the shore and brings buckets of sand back home to bury his brother Goper. Then, when Morv isn't looking, Goper bashes him in the back of the head with a brick until he speaks in foreign languages and can no longer taste. Then they scamper off to grab a sandwich.

You Will Need

- ✪ The Basic Creature Sewing Kit (page 9)
- ✪ 2 crew socks
- ✪ Supplies for 2 pairs of Nice to T You eyes (page 32)
- ✪ Swatches of sock material for teeth and tongues (page 36)

Cutting Out Your Parts

The cutting for this project should be pretty simple. See **figure 1** for a quick diagram. Each of the hacked-off toe segments provides one arm and one row of spikes, and the rest of the sock provides the face and body for the twins. See **figure 2** for an overview of parts.

Take both bodies and lay them flat on their backs with the heels facing upward. Even everything out so that the heels are in the middle and there are no twists or wrinkles. See **figure 3**. Cut a chunk from the cuff of both bodies, and cut straight up the edge of the sock on the side from where you cut the chunk. Stop this cut roughly 2 to 3 inches (5.1 to 7.6 cm) below the heel. Make sure the chunks of cuff you cut out are equal in size and shape, and mirror one another. They should be less than half the width of the socks, but not by much.

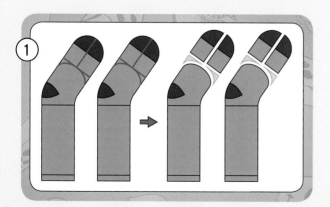

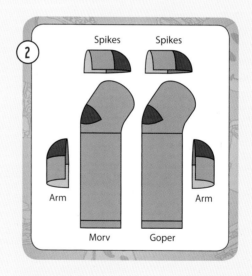

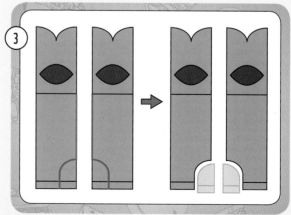

Sewing Morv & Goper

Once the bodies are de-chunked and sliced up the side, turn Goper wrong side out. Shove a right-side-out Morv all the way up inside Goper, matching the two socks at the cuts you made in their sides **(figure 4)**. Pin and stitch the edges together as shown in the diagram. Leave a 3-inch (7.6 cm) length of space unstitched in the back side of the seam (the nonheel side) for turning and stuffing.

When that's done, pull Morv outside of Goper, making both twins wrong side out. See **figure 5**. Pin and stitch the crotch and legs into round little feet as shown. Trim and notch (see page 16) the seam allowance where necessary.

Put the twins down for a bit and turn your attention to the spikes. Follow **figure 6** for the next steps. Grab one of the toe segments you cut for a row of spikes. Turn it wrong side out. Pin and stitch a line in the shape of the spikes you want. Try to keep the bottom points of the spikes a good ⅜ to ½ inch (.95 to 1.3 cm) away from the open edges of your sock part. Trim and notch the seam allowances around your spikes. Turn the row of spikes right side out and topstitch a seam ¼ inch (.6 cm) from the sewn edge of the spikes to stabilize the shape. Repeat these steps for the other row of spikes.

It's time to attach the spikes to the heads. What you need to do is insert the spikes, points first, into the guys' heads as shown in **figure 7**. Match the edge of the spikes with the open edges of the head. If the spikes are longer than the opening in the head, you can gently stretch the opening to accommodate the spikes, or cut the opening a tad larger. Pin and stitch the head closed, clamping the spikes into place.

When both rows of spikes are stitched into place, turn the twins right side out through the hole in their back. Stuff them thoroughly through that hole and close it up with a ladder stitch.

Grab the parts you cut for the twins' arms and turn them wrong side out. Follow the instructions for Jabby Hands on page 27 of the Basics section to transform those sock bits into arms **(figure 8)**. Stuff the arms thoroughly, but leave ¼ inch (.6 cm) of space unstuffed at the open edge.

Use a ladder stitch to attach the arms to the body wherever you think the arms should go **(figure 9)**.

Follow the instructions for Nice to T You eyes on page 32 of the Basics section, or find another solution for the eyes you want your twins to have. Use the instructions for the Signature Stupid Sock Creature Mouth on page 32 to sculpt boofy, poofy lips for your guys. If you want teeth, find instructions for those on page 36, and take care of that before you sculpt the lips.

And there you have it. If you know a pair of less-than-bright twins, maybe give your two-headed creature to them as a gift. Perhaps like their brain, they'll trade off days playing with it. Otherwise, let your twins run around the house intending chaos. Likely your china is safe, since most of the time Morv and Goper are just too dense to know how chaos is properly done. Try conjoining them back to back. They'd make great friends for Give and Take (page 46). Have fun!

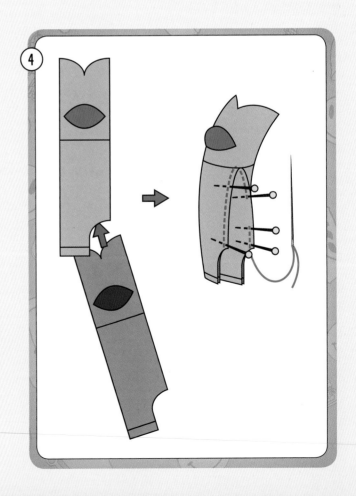

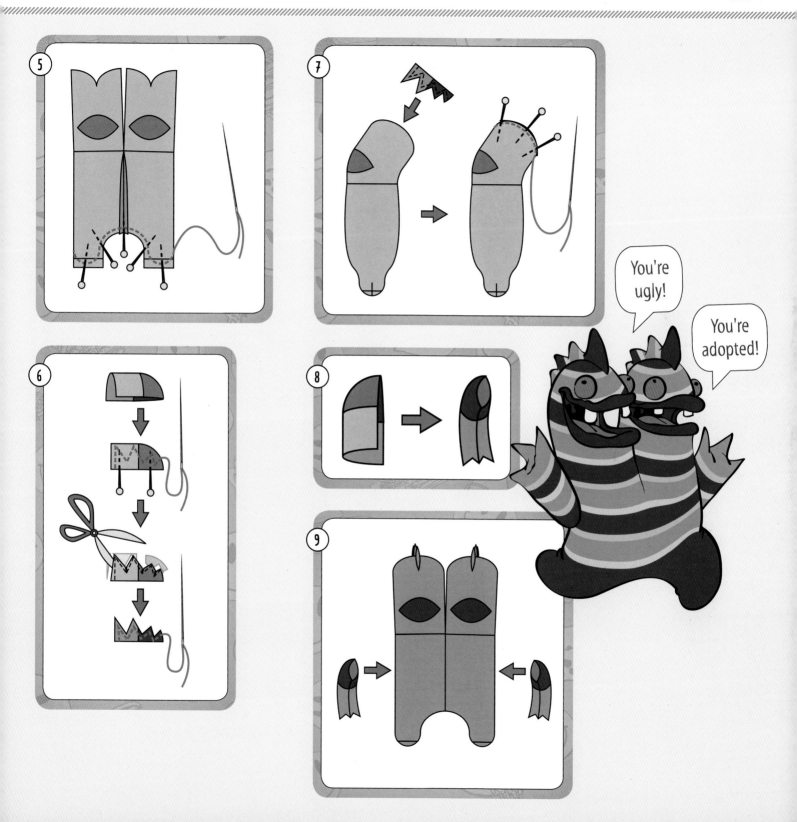

by Audrey Farrell

GLENSPHIRE

The Glensphires are an evolutionary mystery for sure. They burrow underground in an advanced array of tunnels often mistaken for rabbit holes or those of large snakes, which helps keep the Glensphire species obscure.

You Will Need

- ✪ The Basic Creature Sewing Kit (page 9)
- ✪ 2 crew socks with heels
- ✪ Spare material such as felt or fleece for add-ons, foot patches, and a tongue
- ✪ Supplies for Pongscription Lenses (page 30)

Cutting Out Your Parts

Have a look at the cut marks in **figure 1** and imitate them onto your own pair of socks. This project will be a tad different from the others as far as cutting goes, so look lively.

The foot and heel of your first sock will be the head for your Glensphire. The tube of that sock will become the underside of his legs; note that you cut the tube off and slice it up one edge to make a big, flat rectangle of fabric. A section of the second sock including the heel and roughly half the tube will become

the top side of the Glensphire's three legs. You'll need to cut this section off the sock and create three flaps of equal width in the tube. **Figure 2** will show you what this piece needs to look like.

In addition to the parts your socks will yield, you'll need to make a tongue for your Glensphire. Find instructions for that on page 37 of the Basics section. You can make the eyes now or when prompted later in the project.

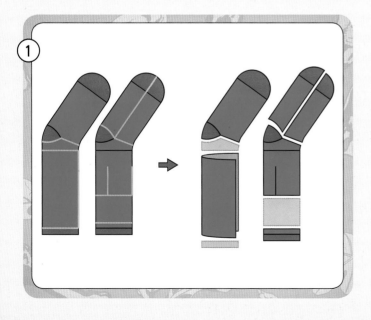

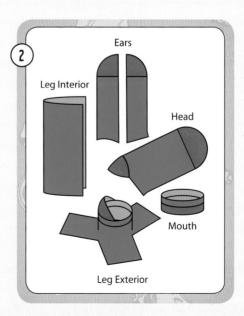

Sewing Glensphire

We'll get the legs out of the way first since they're probably the most unusual feature. Grab the leg interior and lay it flat with the right side up. Turn the leg exterior wrong side out and arrange the three leg flaps even and flat onto the leg interior. If the legs overhang the edges of the interior, trim them evenly. Pin the pieces into place, and trim the interior rectangle to match the leg exteriors. Stitch the sides of the legs together, leaving the feet open for adding footpads later. Notch and trim (see page 16) the seam allowances where necessary **(figure 3)**.

Turn the legs right side out. Turn the head wrong side out. Shove the legs, feet first, down into the head. Match the open edges of both parts, aligning the heels together. Stitch these edges together, leaving a 2-inch (5.1 cm) opening at the heels for turning and stuffing **(figure 4)**.

Let that body breathe for a second and turn your attention to ears. These will be some of the easiest ears you'll ever make in this book, but trust me, they look great. Sometimes long and floppy is just what the doctor ordered (or what the dinosaurs spawned with the donkeys). Fold each ear wrong side out, and stitch the long, straight edge **(figure 5)**. It's that easy. Trim the seam allowance at the tip of the ear to eliminate bunching when you turn the ear right side out.

Next, you'll need to make slits for attaching the ears and the mouth. Grab your Glensphire's body and keep it wrong side out. Make horizontal slits in the head where you'd like the ears to go. Carefully cut one ear slit at a time through only one layer of the sock. Next, cut a slit in the edge of the underside of the head where you want the mouth to go **(figure 6)**.

Turn the ears right side out, and insert them, tip first, into the slits in your Glensphire's head. Use the slit method from page 22 of the Basics section to attach these ears. Grab the tongue you made and tuck it into the cut you created for the mouth. Align the cut edges of both those items. Insert these pieces into the slit you cut in the underside of the Glensphire's head. Use the slit method to attach the mouth features. See **figure 7** for details.

The last thing you have to do to complete the body of your Glensphire is to attach the footpads. Cut three circles from the spare material you selected. Make them half ½ inch (1.3 cm) larger in diameter than the openings of the Glensphire's feet to accommodate a seam allowance. Stitch them on to the openings of the feet, and there you go **(figure 8)**.

Turn your Glensphire right side out through the opening you left at his heel-made humpback. Stuff him till he's the firmness you like. Stitch him shut using a ladder stitch, which is explained on page 18. Make Pongscription Lenses eyes for him, according to the instructions on page 30, or choose from one of the other eye options, if you want.

Stick your Glensphire in a backpack and take it to the zoo. See if it shows more of an affinity to the beasts of burden or to those lizards that never move no matter how hard you tap the glass. Learn from these techniques and see what other unheard-of crossbreeds you can design on your own.

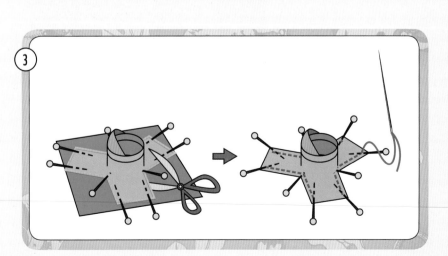

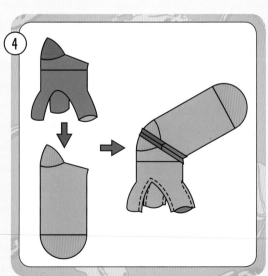

Time for a kiss!

by John Murphy

JERRY JEROME

Jerry Jerome fell on his head as a young boy and since then has thought that every Tuesday is a holiday. It threw him for a loop when he visited all the party supply stores in town to discover not a single "Happy Tuesday" item.

You Will Need

- ✪ The Basic Creature Sewing Kit (page 9)
- ✪ 2 crew socks
- ✪ Supplies for Nice to T You eyes (page 32)

Cutting Out Your Parts

Alright. You need to see **figure 1** for diagrams on cutting your socks, and **figure 2** shows what parts each of your cuts should have produced. The first sock provides Jerry Jerome's body and ears. The second will give you his face, tummy, tail, and arms.

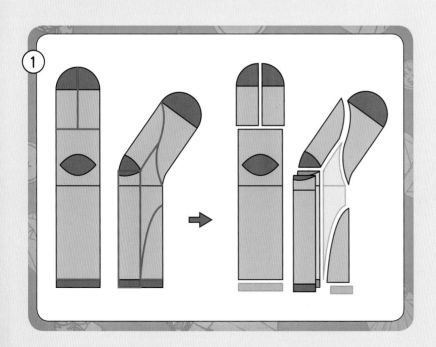

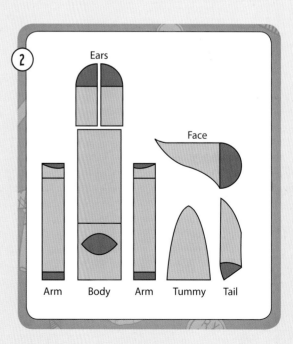

Sewing Jerry Jerome

Would you believe that Jerry Jerome's stitching actually begins with more cutting? See **figure 3**, and round off the top of Jerry Jerome's body as shown. Make sure that as you do this, the heel is toward the bottom half of the body. When you've rounded those corners, cut 1 inch (2.5 cm) or so down both edges, and turn the body wrong side out. You may need to trim more on the edge of the heel side of the sock, but you'll cross that bridge if and when. Grab the toe part you cut for Jerry Jerome's face, and insert it as shown into the top of the body. You'll want to match the midpoint at the edge of the toe to the vertex of the cut at the edge of Jerry Jerome's body. Pin the toe into place.

Pin the edges of Jerry Jerome's face to the rounded top edges of his body as shown in **figure 4**. Match the edges only to the midpoint of the curve, which is essentially the very top of Jerry Jerome's body. Stitch the edges you've matched thus far. Reference instructions for the vee method on page 22 if any of this confuses you.

Prepare to use the vee method again to attach the ears. Take the parts of the sock toe you cut for Jerry Jerome's ears, and place a pin right at the middle of the bottom edge. Tuck that pinned edge right into the corner where you stopped stitching the edges of the face and the body **(figure 5)**. Match the bottom edge of the ear to the edges of the face and the body as shown in **figure 6**. Stitch those edges together.

When that's done to both ears, draw them out of the body. Match the ends of the seams where they connect to the face and the body. Match the unsewn edges of the ears, and continue matching the edges of the face to the edges of the body. If you need to extend the cut at the back of the head to fit the rest of the face, do so little by little until everything fits just right. Pin as necessary, and stitch from the tops of the ears to the corner of the cut at the back of the body **(figure 7)**.

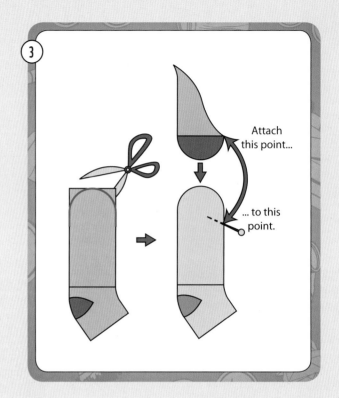

3

Attach this point...

... to this point.

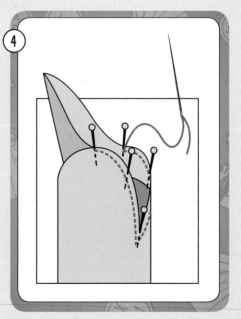

4

Keep the body wrong side out, and lay it flat on its back. Cut a slit in the front layer of the body long enough to fit the tummy **(figure 8)**. Use the vee method again to attach the tummy to the body. When you've done that, stitch two round foot shapes in the bottom of the body, but don't stitch up the crotch. You'll need that open for stuffing. Trim the corners of the feet as necessary.

Take the part you cut for Jerry Jerome's tail and turn it wrong side out. Stitch up the open edges as shown in **figure 9**. Then snip and pry a hole in Jerry Jerome's butt where you think his tail ought to go. Attach the tail using the circumference method, which you can find described on page 21 **(figure 10)**. When the tail is attached, turn Jerry Jerome right side out and stuff him thoroughly.

The last parts you need to make for Jerry Jerome are his arms. Grab the strips of sock material you cut for his arms and follow the Grabby Hands instructions from page 29. When you've done that, stuff them thoroughly **(figure 11)**.

Use a ladder stitch to attach Jerry Jerome's arms to his body where you think they ought to go **(figure 12)**.

Follow the instructions for the Signature Stupid Sock Creature Mouth found on page 32. You'll find his lips might be a tad more boofy than other creatures with that mouth, because his lips are made from a toe. I used the Nice to T You eyes for Jerry Jerome; you can find those instructions on page 32. If you decide an alternate eye is best for your creature, have at it. I won't sue you.

And there you are. Happy Tuesday! Make sure you celebrate.

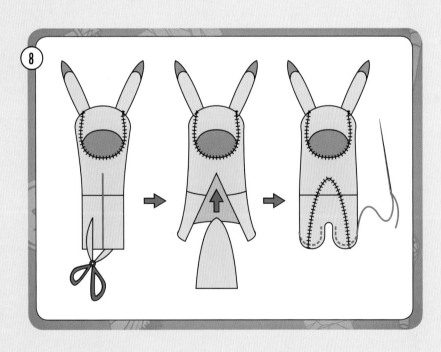

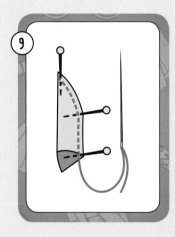

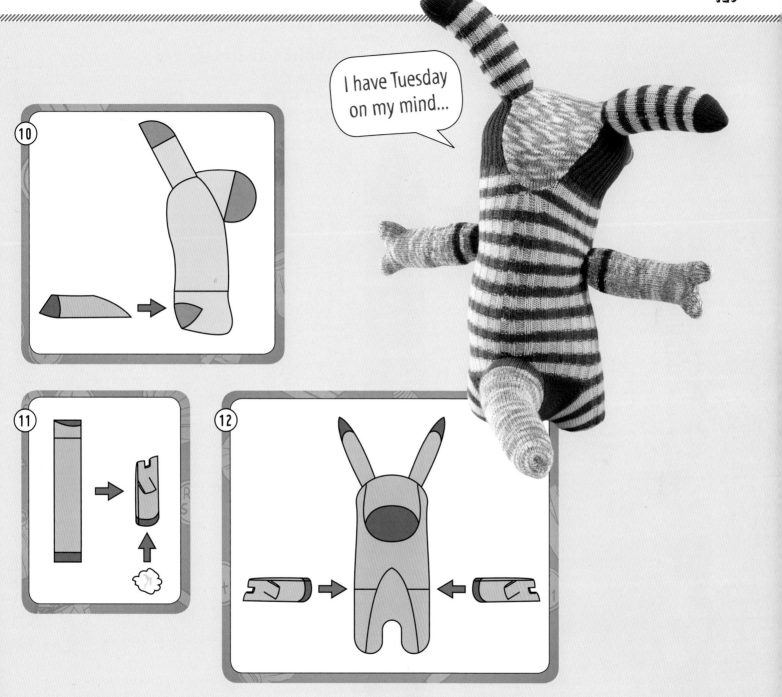

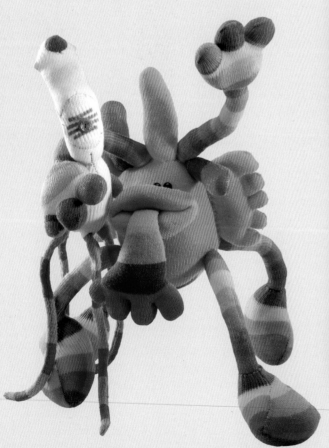

About the Designers

Jennifer Brett, mother of twins, is a social media director from the Philadelphia area. She studied fine art photography at Syracuse University and has shown in galleries across the United States.

Ian Dennis is John Murphy's former studio assistant and a monster-making genius. He sells used books online and teaches ceramic sculpture to young children in Winston-Salem, North Carolina.

Audrey Farrell, from Hamilton, New York, started making sock monsters as a fourth grader. Now a seventh grader, she sells her creatures at the local farmers' market and is saving to buy a new flute.

Jamie Harris is an English teacher turned librarian from the Las Vegas Valley. She started making sock creatures after she saw the *Stupid Sock Creatures* kit in her local quilt store; she plans to continue growing as a fiber artist.

Graham Scott Holt currently resides in Arlington, Massachusetts. Aside from making sock creatures, he enjoys cooking, candy making, and working in the garden with his wife, Nicole, without whom Graham's creations would lack color direction and a sense of completion.

Kittypinkstars is recreating her home planet one long-legged creature at a time, thanks to imagination and a *big* sock drawer! With a passion for making stuff, Kitty is terraforming the globe with her rainbow-colored sock creatures.

Nate Little is a California-based artist and designer. Born and raised in SoCal, he grew up visiting Disneyland and keeping his vivid imagination active. You can see his latest creations at his website www.MadArtisanLabs.com.

By day, Elizabeth "Lizapest" Mielke, is a registered early childhood educator (ECE) from Toronto, Ontario. By night, she is a serial creator in a multitude of disciplines, such as paper, fiber, socks, and ukulele.

Kelly McCaffrey, daughter of a doll maker, is no stranger to handmade clothes and soft sculpture dolls. After a lifetime of experimenting with sock monkeys, she tried her hand at *Stupid Sock Creatures* and now produces a menagerie of extraordinary toys.

John Murphy created the Stupid Creatures™ sock monsters on a whim in 2003. Since then, he has enjoyed nearly a decade making plush monsters, writing about them, and teaching people to make them. He currently works in his home state of North Carolina as a counselor for at-risk kids and their families, and he hopes to never stop. Visit www.stupidcreatures.com to learn more.

Kathryn Odell believes in play. As a substitute teacher, she brings play into the classroom on a regular basis. When she's not teaching, you will find her deeply involved in many kinds of craft.

Addicus Patton is a sailor and a very influential sock-creature maker. He has made his fair share of sock monsters, taught people how to make them, and even left a few as souvenirs on naval vessels.

Lise Petrauskas, an award-winning sock-monster maker from Portland, Oregon, is the founder of La Société des Monstres Célèbres. She initiated an international holiday for monsters and those who love them. Her creations can be seen at www.societedesmonstres.com.

UK native **Louise Revill** is the founder of Odd Sox (www. facebook.com/oddsoxrox), a sock monster phenomenon with its own following. She says this of making sock monsters: "Once you've made your first, there's no going back!"

Ed Saul, from Gloucestershire and Canterbury, United Kingdom, likes books, drinks tea, wrestles crustaceans, and sews socks. He's available for all parties, shindigs, barn dances, and box socials after 11 o'clock as long as someone else buys the drinks.

Evan Summers, 16, is a vigilante, insomniac rabble-rouser who hails from Springfield, Tennessee. A musician, cartoonist, toy maker, and amateur witch doctor, Evan writes music for his band, Reptile Dysfunction, and captures ghosts in his free time.

Acknowledgments

The following people have all influenced how this book turned out, so hopefully it sells like mad. A big thank you goes out to my perturbing and outstanding former campers, the Kahulyas, who gave me unexpected purpose and direction. Thanks also to my editor, Thom O'Hearn, who extended nearly all of my deadlines. I couldn't have done this book without my team of exceptional designers: Lizapest, Jamie, Jen, Kathryn, Audrey, Louise, Lise, Graham, Kelly, Ed, Nate, Kittypinkstars, Evan, Addicus, and Ian. Their dedication, enthusiasm, and projects made this thing you're reading a reality. Thanks to readers like Carmen, Clarita, Eileen, Darcy, Maggie, Dakoda, Jeff, and Vivian, who gave constant support, friendship, and affirmation. And of course, a big helping of thanks and love for my weird family. They let me visit anytime and keep ice cream in the freezer. This book is dedicated to Martha Barton. If there are bookshelves in Heaven, Mimmaw, I hope you can find a copy of this.

Index